T0339070

KARL MARX'S
CAPITAL
AND THE PRESENT
Four Essays

KARL MARX'S
CAPITAL
AND THE PRESENT
Four Essays

C.P. CHANDRASEKHAR

Foreword by
Prabhat Patnaik

 Tulika Books

Published by
Tulika Books
44, first floor, Shahpur Jat, New Delhi 110 049, India
www.tulikabooks.in

First edition (hardback) 2017

ISBN: 978-81-93401-56-9

Printed at Chaman Offset, Delhi 110 002

For
RAJEN
steadfast friend and guide

Contents

Foreword

PRABHAT PATNAIK

Marxism is famously said to have three sources and three component parts: classical German philosophy, French socialism, English classical political economy. While basing itself upon these three, however, it also at the same time decisively *broke* with each of them. But while its break with classical German philosophy has been much discussed, as indeed its break with French socialism, its break in the realm of political economy has scarcely received the attention it deserves. The fact that the renowned economist Paul Samuelson, admittedly not sympathetic to Marxism, could dismiss Marx as a 'minor post-Ricardian' suggests a lack of awareness about the Ricardo–Marx, or rather the Smith–Ricardo–Marx, relationship that is quite staggering. And this in turn testifies to how little the matter has been discussed in the literature.

The tendency among non-Marxists has been to focus mainly on Marx's value-theoretic discussion, and to reinterpret Marx's 'prices of production' in terms of Piero Sraffa's analysis of equilibrium prices in his *Production of Commodities by Means of Commodities*. Since Sraffa's work in this sphere

has been taken as vindicating Ricardo's approach to the determination of 'natural prices', the net result of this entire discussion has been to obliterate rather than underscore the distance
between Marx and Ricardo. The issue of price determination
has also absorbed much attention among Marxists themselves, who have correspondingly devoted less time than they
should have to discussing the *distance* between Marx and his
classical predecessors.

On this issue of distance, what Marx himself had said in
his time continues more or less to be the basic position among
most Marxists. According to Marx this distance, it may be
recalled, lay in two inter-related areas: the perception of history and the theory of surplus value. There were, of course,
important specific differences, such as on the possibility of
generalized overproduction and on the theory of ground rent.
But the tendency among most Marxists has been to believe
that if we leave aside such differences on specific issues and
focus only on the basic perspectival differences, then these
two inter-related areas are the main point of demarcation.

This book, containing four lectures delivered by Professor
C.P. Chandrasekhar under the auspices of Sahmat (Safdar
Hashmi Memorial Trust) on the occasion of the 150th anniversary of the publication of *Das Kapital*, assumes importance
in this context: not only does the author discuss this issue
of distance directly, but, by bringing the Marxist analysis of
capitalism up to date and throwing light on the current era of
finance capital, he implicitly emphasizes the rich potential of
Marxism which sets it apart from classical political economy.
The differences between Marx and classical political economy,
as he notes, were far more profound; the distance travelled by
Marx away from classical political economy was far greater

than is commonly presumed. But before we come to that, let us recapitulate these two basic differences.

In *The Poverty of Philosophy*, Marx criticizes classical political economy for its perception that till now there has been history but henceforth there will be none – i.e. for its perception of capitalism as the end of history; as an economic order in conformity with human nature, and with nature in general, for the achievement of which the entire preceding history had acted as a backdrop. There is here a remarkable parallel between this view of classical political economy and that of Hegelian philosophy, which also saw the climax of history in the arrival of the Prussian state. The concepts used by classical political economy, such as 'natural price', 'natural rate of profit' and the like, are simply reminders of its position that the categories of capitalism are indeed 'natural' categories, that this economic system is in conformity with nature.

Marx, in contrast, saw it as an exploitative system, just as slavery and feudalism before it had been. It was exploitative not in terms of any Lockean 'natural rights' doctrine but on a par with other preceding modes of production in history, where a surplus was extracted from the direct producers by a class of non-producers. Far from representing the end of history, therefore, capitalism needed to be transcended if mankind had to proceed from what Marx called its pre-history, to which capitalism as an exploitative system also belonged, to its real history which it would make consciously through its praxis. History, in short, did not end with the beginning of capitalism; instead, history began with the end of capitalism.

The question before Marx, therefore, was how to unearth the manner of exploitation under capitalism when the relations in the capitalist marketplace were governed by voluntary contracts and there was an exchange of equivalents. And this led to his second basic difference from classical political economy, namely his theory of surplus value, which was part of the problematic rooted in his perspective on history. Classical political economy no doubt had occasionally shown a dim awareness of the fact of exploitation under capitalism, such as when Smith had advanced his 'deduction theory of profits', or Ricardo had seen profits as a surplus or (in De Quincy's words) as the 'leavings of wages'. But why such a surplus arose is a matter that was never pursued.

In fact the Malthusian theory of population, according to which the supply of labour adjusted to the demand for it at a subsistence wage so that any increase in wages above subsistence level created an excess supply of labour that drove wages down to subsistence, provided a readymade explanation for the existence of a surplus that came to capitalists. But this only suggested that the fact of the surplus coming to capitalists was the result of *a failing on the part of the workers themselves*, namely, their propensity to procreate excessively the moment they climbed out of a subsistence level of living. (Marx, not surprisingly, was to call the Malthusian theory of population a 'libel on the human race'.)

The investigation into the mode of extraction of the surplus, which under capitalism took the form of surplus value, led Marx, as is well known, to his seminal discoveries: the distinction between labour and labour power; the identification of the sphere of production as the location where surplus value was generated; the two-fold nature of labour, abstract and concrete labour, corresponding to the two-fold nature of commodities, as exchange value and use value; the pervasive dualism that characterized all categories under capitalism, where a product was simultaneously a commodity, the labour process simultaneously a value-creating process, the surplus simultaneously surplus value; and so on. Chandrasekhar, in his first lecture, gives an extremely lucid account of these seminal discoveries of Marx.

'Historicizing Ricardo', in short, did not mean just adding a historical sequel to capitalism, with which classical political economy thought that history had come to an end; nor did it mean offering just an ethical critique of the capitalist system, leaving its analysis as undertaken by Ricardo untouched (as the Ricardian socialists like Hodgkin had done). *It meant a completely different analysis of capitalism*, which in turn opened up new areas for investigation. How did labour power become a commodity? (Here Marx was inspired by, and turned upside down, a Smithian concept – 'the original accumulation of capital' – to propound his own concept of the 'primitive accumulation of capital'.) How are the social relations that create capital and wage labour reproduced over time? How does a surplus value continue to get extracted since the Malthusian theory of population does not hold? (Here Marx advanced one of his most insightful concepts, the reserve army of labour.) And so on. The reader gets a flavour of all this from Chandrasekhar's book.

Capitalism, as the author underscores following Marx, is not just an exploitative system; it is also an anarchic system. A major source of anarchy is the fact that capitalists' investment decisions are uncoordinated. The aggregate amount of investment thrown up by such uncoordinated decisions, therefore, may be insufficient to permit realization of the entire unconsumed surplus value at normal capacity output (workers more or less consume what they get as wages), which is the cause of a crisis (though Marx, as the author rightly says, did not have just one single theory of crisis). The differences between

Tugan-Baranovsky and Rosa Luxemburg are discussed by the author along the way, together with imperialism, the role of the state, the so-called 'Golden Age of Capitalism' and its coming to an end, and the emergence of finance to a position of ascendancy. The role of finance in shoring up demand through credit-sustained booms is highlighted by the author, though, as he rightly says, this can only be a temporary palliative, as the contemporary crisis of capitalism clearly demonstrates.

II

Capitalism, however, is not just an exploitative and anarchic system. It is also a *spontaneous* system. And a crucial difference between classical political economy and Marx lies in the latter's asserting this fact, which does not just elude the former but constitutes an antithesis to the latter's discourse. Classical political economy's starting point was the individual. Interactions between individuals without any interference by the state produced an outcome different from what the individuals themselves had visualized or intended: it produced economic progress. Hence, while the Hegelian dictum that 'the whole is not the sum of the parts' was accepted by classical political economy, this dictum was used in support of *laissez-faire*. Notwithstanding Smith's aversion to Mandeville's idea of 'private vices' producing 'public virtue', his own 'invisible hand' suggested something similar. The political pogramme that classical economics generated was for a liberal order.

Marx, too, accepted the Hegelian dictum that the whole was not the mere sum of parts; but in building up the whole, he saw the individual not as the starting point but as an entity itself constituted by the coercion exercised by the capitalist order, which pitted one economic participant against another in a competitive struggle. A capitalist accumulates not because he likes to do so but because he is engaged in a Darwinian struggle with his competitors and would fall by the wayside if he did not continuously introduce technological change, for which he needs capital on a growing scale that only accumulation can put at his command. Capitalism, in short, was a system where each 'economic agent' occupied a position from which he would get displaced if he did not act in a particular way that the system demanded of him. Marx, interestingly, as the author notes, had called the capitalist 'capital personified'; i.e. the individuality of the capitalist, his volitions, were of little relevance.

The net outcome of each 'agent' acting in this manner was a movement that gave rise to a set of immanent tendencies of the system, which constituted its 'spontaneity'. Interference with such immanent tendencies made the system dysfunctional, necessitating either further and further interference that, if allowed to proceed, would ultimately lead to its transcendence, or a rolling back of the original act of interference itself. (Needless to say, the only interference the system could accept was one that was congruent with and hastened the immanent tendencies themselves.)

The political agenda that necessarily followed from this conception of a 'spontaneous order' was socialism. If capitalism could be a malleable system, if it could be 'reformed' through keeping its spontaneous tendencies at bay, then there would be little need for transcending it. But precisely because it was characterized by spontaneity, and hence by *generalized* alienation (including of the capitalists), human freedom demanded that this spontaneous system be overthrown; that it be replaced by one where the people could collectively shape their own destiny, including their economic lives, by effecting an economic order that made the economy subject to politics rather than the other way around.

It was therefore not just a conception of history or a recognition of exploitation under capitalism that distinguished Marx from classical political economy; it was a conception of capitalism itself that, far from seeing it as the means of achieving individuality and freedom, saw it, because of its spontaneity, as a universally alienating system that stood in the way of *both*. The pursuit of the socialist project did not involve a question of collectivism *versus* individualism, as Hayek was to put it later, *but of individualism itself, which could be reclaimed through collective praxis.* This was the distance between classical political economy and Marx, who had 'inverted' not only Hegel but Adam Smith as well.

III

One of the immanent tendencies of capitalism highlighted by Marx is centralization of capital which, Lenin had argued, gave rise to finance capital, a coalescence of banking and industrial capital that was presided over by a financial oligarchy. The finance capital that Lenin had analysed was 'national', linked to a particular nation-state and engaged in rivalry for 'economic territory' with the finance capitals of other 'nations' within the metropolis, which were also backed by their own respective nation-states. Further centralization since Lenin's time, however, has given rise today to an *international* finance capital which is globally mobile in quest of capital gains and has erected an enormous superstructure of finance, whose analysis has thrown up a number of questions for Marxist theory. The author's discussion of these questions is a crucial aspect of the book and is extremely illuminating.

Marx had seen all incomes accruing to financiers, who were the source of interest-bearing capital, as arising from the surplus value extracted from the workers. The total surplus value extracted from the workers, in other words, was shared between the different segments of property owners, in the form of rent, interest and profits. He had even seen this comprehensive view of the origin of different strands of property income, instead of their being treated as independent streams, as marking the superiority of his own theory over classical political economy. But what is the source of the financial earnings that are so extraordinarily large in the present times? The initial answer would be that such earnings arise not from surplus value but from capital gains. This, however, begs the question: since capital gains cannot accrue *ad infinitum* to all financial asset-holders, a large part of such earnings must then be simply notional or fictitious, in which case the capital supposedly fetching such earnings must also be fictitious.

Questions such as these have never been satisfactorily answered. The merit of this book is that Chandrasekhar provides a clear, brilliant and unambiguous answer to this question; and the answer simply is that such earnings in general are *not fictitious*. Obviously, not all such earnings come out of the produced surplus value, but those that do not represent either gains at the expense of pre-capitalist producers whose assets are being continuously expropriated through a process of primitive accumulation of capital; or claims upon the current or future revenues of the state, i.e. gains at the expense of the working people immediately or in the future; or claims over future property which hitherto non-appropriated elements of nature – such as water, air, common land, forests or air-waves – are going to be turned into. What appears at first sight fictitious, in other words, is very real in the sense of representing claims upon future property.

One conclusion that can be drawn from Chandrasekhar's analysis is that the process of so-called 'financialization' hastens the process of commoditization and hence private appropriation, of common resources of nature which have been hitherto enjoyed *gratis* by mankind. The implications of this phenomenon are enormous and obviously sinister.

IV

An important feature of the book is an analysis of the dialectics of anarchy and order within capitalism. While anarchy is a perennial feature of the system and underlies its proneness to crises (Keynes too was later to highlight anarchy as underlying 'involuntary unemployment'), the system does after all function *through such crises*. It has, in other words, an order that is fashioned out of such anarchy. The system achieves an order of sorts through such anarchy, an example of which is the fact that the crisis itself, by destroying existing capital, recreates the condition for the process of accumulation of capital to resume.

Marx, in *Capital*, saw the capitalist system as a closed, isolated system, operating under its own immanent tendencies and fashioning by its inner logic an order out of its anarchy. While he was extremely sensitive to the issue of colonialism and imperialism, and wrote with extraordinary insight about its impact on colonized societies, its role in the dynamics of the colonizing economy did not figure much in his writings (except in the posthumously published Volume III of *Capital* where it figures among the 'counteracting tendencies' to the falling tendency of the rate of profit).

Marx took over the picture of a closed capitalist economy from classical political economy. Even though classical political economy did not have any notion of a crisis while Marx did, he saw a resolution of the crisis occurring within this closed capitalist system itself. This view, however, is neither theoretically robust nor historically accurate. It is theoretically doubtful because the scrapping of capital stock, which Marx saw as ending the crisis, can even worsen the crisis, since the firms that go out of business because of such scrapping (which, incidentally, is the mechanism of centralization) also stop spending when they go out of business; and this reduces demand as well. Scrapping, in short, affects both the supply and demand sides, and there is no reason why supplies should be more reduced than demand, thereby causing a revival of capacity utilization and hence accumulation.

The mechanism through which Marx saw the crisis as ending within a closed capitalist system, in other words, does not necessarily work even at a theoretical level. And in practice, as is well known, the means of getting out of crises in the 'long nineteenth century' was encroaching into colonial markets rather than any automatic rise in capacity utilization through a scrapping of existing equipment.

The contradiction between anarchy and order within the capitalist system was thus resolved through colonialism rather than through the mere inner working of a closed capitalist economy, as Marx suggests. In fact, a good deal of what is attributed to the functioning of the 'market' is really a result of the system's coupling with outlying regions that were forcibly brought under its sway. Imperialism, in short, played the role that is often attributed, following Smith, to the 'invisible hand'.

Marx became more aware of the crucial role of imperialism in the functioning of capitalism towards the end of his life. Thus, in a letter to Danielson on 19 February 1881, Marx had talked of the 'economic drain' from India in the following words: 'What the English take from them annually . . . without any equivalent and quite apart from what they appropriate to themselves annually within India . . . amounts to more than the total sum of income of the sixty millions of agricultural and industrial labourers of India.' A 'drain' of this order of magnitude could not have been unimportant for the dynamics of British capitalism, and hence of the system as a whole. Marx, alas, did not have time to incorporate it into his analysis, but it would be odd for Marxists today not to recognize its role and merely to repeat Marx's analysis in *Capital* as the final word on the subject. The author's lucid and insightful presentation in this book opens up the possibility for productive discussion on many of these themes.

Acknowledgements

I am thankful to the Safdar Hashmi Memorial Trust (Sahmat) for inviting me to deliver these four lectures, organized under its auspices to mark the 150th anniversary of the publication of the first German edition of *Capital*, Volume 1. I have benefited immensely from detailed discussions with Prabhat Patnaik and Jayati Ghosh in the course of writing these lectures. I also had the benefit of comments from Venkatesh Athreya, Akeel Bilgrami, T. Jayaraman, Sashi Kumar, Utsa Patnaik, Rajendra Prasad, N. Ram, Abhijit Sen, Jahnavi Sen, C.S.R. Shankar, Chandradutt Thalikulam and Nobuharu Yokogawa. Responses from those who attended these lectures are also gratefully acknowledged. None of them, however, is responsible for the final form the lectures have taken.

KARL MARX'S
CAPITAL
AND THE PRESENT

1

Das Kapital and the Critique of Bourgeois Political Economy

We mark the 150th anniversary of the publication of the first German edition of *Capital* not just because it is a seminal text of historical interest, but to celebrate a treatise that has had a major influence on those who have, over these 150 years, tried to understand the nature of capitalism and its dynamics. It is a text that has shaped the ideological moorings of a major section of movements of the workers and the peasantry, for whom it was the equivalent of the Bible for the devout Christian, as Engels claimed it was for the working class on the continent in the late nineteenth century.[1] It is also a text that provides us with the essentials of a method that helps extend and contemporize the analysis in *Capital* itself – in sum, a living text with an abiding influence.

For these reasons, in the 150 years since the publication of the first German edition of *Das Kapital*, the three volumes of this seminal work have been 'read' and interpreted many

---

[1] Karl Marx, *Capital: A Critique of Political Economy* (*Das Kapital* series, Book 1), Penguin Books, Kindle edition, 1976, p. 112.

times over, with each reading influenced by the social, economic and political conditions of the time. That is the way it must be for a text that is as much a political testament as it is a treatise on economics. Indeed Marx himself was clear that developments in political economy were influenced by the historical context in which they arose, by the level of development of and contradictions characterizing the real economy of the relevant time. Hence, when we return to *Capital* today, it is not merely to understand its method and substance, but to use Marx's method to assess the transformation of capitalism since his time – while recognizing that this transformation itself influences our reading of his analysis of capitalism and determines how we apply it to the present.

A reading of many of the writings of Marx and Engels stretching over the period from the publication of *The Communist Manifesto* to the publication of *Capital* lends credence to the idea that they would have been dismissive of any suggestion that 150 years after the publication of *Capital*, Volume 1, Marx's analysis would be of more than historical interest. They clearly believed that the rapid development of productive forces evidenced by capitalism in England, the inevitable barriers to that process set by the social relations that defined capitalism, the crises that the anarchy of capitalism as a system would engender, and the fact that the emergence and growth of the capitalist mode had produced its own grave diggers in the form of the working class, would result in the transcendence of capitalism in not too distant a future. The 'revolutions' of 1847–48 were missed opportunities, but the inevitable periodic crises of capitalism would ensure a shift away from the system.

This perception has implicit in it the idea that the 'progressive' character of capitalism would be its undoing, with technological change turning the social relations that unleashed them into fetters. A consequence of this perception was that alongside a discussion of the ways in which the antagonistic relations between capital and labour shaped the form and intensity of exploitation, and determined the distribution of income, Marx emphasized the transformative nature of capitalist development. Once the process of primitive accumulation had created the conditions for extraction of surplus value in a system with equivalent exchange, accumulation in its quintessentially capitalist form begins and crudely coercive primitive accumulation moves into the shadows. And once the force of capitalist accumulation unleashes the productive forces, increases in productivity ensure the expansion of surplus product and value, with surplus being extracted in the form of relative surplus value rather than as absolute surplus value, or largely through an extension of the working day and an increase in the intensity of labour. This is sometimes interpreted as an almost linear shift from primitive to normal modes of capital accumulation, and from absolute to relative surplus value extraction. This sense of linearity in the analysis of capitalist development is often read also into Marx's understanding that historical development with transitions through various modes of production occurred because, 'at a certain stage of development the material productive forces of society come into conflict with the existing relations of production or . . . with the property relations within which they have operated hitherto', which 'begins an era of social revolution'.[2] Real history, as Marx himself recognized, is more complex, with

[2] Karl Marx, *A Contribution to the Critique of Political Economy*, Moscow: Progress Publishers, 1970, p. 20 (German edition 1859).

the process characterized not just by distortions but also by periods of reversal.

Yet, this was the process which, in Marx's view, gave rise to capitalism, rendered it transient and prepared the ground for the abolition of private property. Marx built into his analysis three tendencies that made capitalism, like previous modes of production, almost 'inevitably' transient. The first, as already discussed, is the logic of accumulation under capitalism that results in rapid development of the forces of production and brings it into conflict with the social relations of production. In fact Marx went further and saw new forms under capitalism as pointing to a socialization of production, necessitated by concentration and centralization. One such form, the role and impact of which has since proved substantially different, is the joint stock company, which Marx described as reflecting the complete separation of capital ownership from the actual production process, heralding the ownership of enterprise by social capital and an implicit 'abolition of the capitalist mode of production within the capitalist mode of production itself'.[3] The second is the conflict between capital and labour, which cannot be resolved under capitalism, and provides the ground for an overthrow by the working class of the system based on private property and wage labour. And the third is the inevitability of crises under accumulation, which I discuss in the next lecture, that provides the trigger for intensification of class conflict and unleashes revolutionary movements.

[3] Karl Marx, *Capital* (*Das Kapital* series, Book 3), Penguin Books, Kindle edition, 1981, p. 569.

A Critique of Political Economy

Marx framed his discussion in *Capital* as a critique of political economy, especially the works of the 'classical economists' from the Physiocrats through Adam Smith and Ricardo, and in constant opposition to the vulgar economists of that period whom he saw as apologists, conscious or unconscious, for the bourgeoisie. Marx himself dated the beginning of his study of political economy, diverting from his study of jurisprudence that he pursued 'as a subject subordinated to philosophy and history', to 1842–43. In that year, as editor of *Rheinische Zeitung*, he found himself 'in the embarrassing position of having to discuss what are known as material interests', referring to discussions in the Rhenish parliament on forest theft and the division of landed property, the condition of the Moselle peasantry, and debates on free trade and protective tariffs.[4]

Marx did find answers to some of his questions in the work of the classical economists. While appreciative of that work he found it inadequate to his purpose, and intense study led him to an explanation why. Classical political economy, in his view, while associated with and an ideological accompaniment of rising capitalism, belonged to a period in which the class struggle in capitalism was yet underdeveloped. The weakness of that struggle gave the still-nascent bourgeois political economy its scientific perspective, allowing the classical economists to individually contribute many important insights regarding the nature and dynamics of capitalism. These included the identification of productive labour with activity that yielded a surplus product and contributed to accumulation; tracing

---

[4] Marx, *A Contribution to the Critique of Political Economy*, pp. 19–20.

the source of surplus to production rather than circulation;[5] identifying labour time as the ultimate source of value; and recognizing that machinery, even as it enhanced productivity and profits, can displace labour.[6] This inevitably led to a recognition of the antagonism embedded in the capitalist system. However, political economy remained within the bourgeois horizon, 'i.e. in so far as it views the capitalist order as the absolute and ultimate form of social production, instead of as a historically transient stage of development'.[7] According to Marx, even 'its last great representative, David Ricardo, in the end, consistently makes the antagonism of class interests, of wages and profits, of profits and rent, the starting point of his investigation, naively taking the antagonism for a social law of nature.' Hence, in so far as political economy remains within this 'bourgeois horizon', 'it can only remain a science while the class struggle is latent or manifests itself only in isolated and sporadic phenomena',[8] as it had developed till then. And even then, it was in essence merely a science of enrichment that saw such processes of enrichment as the natural order.

Before this turn to political economy, Marx had already made the transition, inspired by his early engagement with

---

[5] But 'Ricardo never concerns himself with the origin of surplus value. He treats it as an entity inherent in the capitalist mode of production, and in his eyes the latter is the natural form of social production. Whenever he discusses the productivity of labour, he seeks in it not the cause of the existence of surplus-value, but the cause that determines the magnitude of that value.' Marx, *Capital: A Critique of Political Economy* (*Das Kapital* series, Book 1), pp. 650–51.

[6] 'It is one of the greatest merits of Ricardo that he saw machinery not only as a means of producing commodities, but also a means of producing a "redundant population".' Ibid., p. 3.

[7] Ibid., p. 96.

[8] Ibid.

young Hegelians, to a radical Republican position with a social dimension. He contrasted the 'Christian state', 'which was an association of believers' and a system that legitimized and protected feudal privileges, with the 'rational state', which converted 'the aims of the individual into general aims, crude instinct into moral inclination, natural independence into spiritual freedom, by the individual finding his good in the life of the whole, and the whole in the frame of mind of the individual'.[9] He was soon convinced that 'legal relations and political forms' 'originate in the material conditions of life, the totality of which Hegel . . . embraces within the term "civil society",' and that 'the anatomy of this civil society' had to be found in political economy.

Seen in this light, Marx's extended engagement with political economy, which began at this time, was part of an effort to combine the application of the Hegelian dialectic – now turned on its head – and the revolutionary ideas derived from the French Revolution and the early Socialists, with an understanding and critique of English political economy. 'English political economy', because it was a progressive 'science' – representing as it did the still progressive capitalism in conflict with the dying feudal order. Critique, because with Ricardo having recognized the conflict between the different class interests, 'the science of bourgeois economy had reached the limits beyond which it cannot pass'.

Nevertheless, Marx clearly believed that its insights, combined with a critique of its inadequate and faulty analysis and limited vision, could take the science in a direction

---

[9] Karl Marx, 'Leading Article in No. 179 of the *Kolnische Zeitung*', 10 July 1842, *MECW*, Vol. 1, p. 189, cited in Gareth Stedman Jones, *Karl Marx: Greatness and Illusion*, London: Allen Lane, 2016, pp. 107–15.

where it became a weapon for the working class. The working class needed this weapon because that class was the instrument through which history would ensure the transcendence of capitalism – a process that bourgeois political economy, which saw capitalism as the end of history, could not contemplate. This perception was in keeping with Marx's adherence to and use of Hegel's dialectic, which, in its rational form,

> includes in its comprehensive and affirmative recognition of the existing state of things, at the same time also, the recognition of the negation of that state, of its inevitable breaking up, because it regards every historically developed social form as in fluid movement, and therefore takes into account its transitional nature not less than its momentary existence, because it lets nothing impose upon it, and is in some sense critical and revolutionary.[10]

Commodities and Capitalism

While classical political economy was his point of departure, Marx's discussion in *Capital* marked a substantial leap forward in several ways. There is the obvious factor of method, where he starts with the elementary form in which wealth appears under capitalism, commodities, to first identify the substance of value, abstract labour time.[11] That in turn gives the magnitudes that define the proportions in which commodities exchange in the market, or their exchange values. While

---

[10] Karl Marx, 'Afterword to Second German Edition', *Capital, Volume 1*, Moscow: Progress Publishers, 1974, p. 29 (German edition 1873).

[11] 'More complex labour counts only as intensified, or rather multiplied simple labour, so that a smaller quantity of complex labour is considered equal to a larger quantity of simple labour.' Marx, *Capital: A Critique of Political Economy* (*Das Kapital* series, Book 1), p. 135.

commodities may be produced and exchanged in different contexts, starting at the borders separating tribal communities and moving to urban centres of a thriving feudal regime, commodity production under capitalism is different for two reasons. First, only such products are best suited to serve as commodities 'as result from different kinds of labour, each being carried out independently and for the account of private individuals'.[12] So, the developed division of labour associated with capitalism universalizes commodity production.

And second, labour power itself appears in the market as a commodity, where the labourer alienates the use value of his capacity to labour and earns its value in exchange. The recognition of the distinction between the labourer and his/her labour power, and between the value of labour power – which is the socially and historically determined cost of reproducing it – and the value that the labourer contributes in the form of living labour during the working day, was the most significant contribution that Marx made to the advance of political economy. That helped identify the source of surplus value in a world of exchange of equivalents, and transform the analysis of capitalism and its dynamic. A capitalist who has bought the right to the use value of labour power, which he has paid for at its value, acquires the right to the surplus value that is congealed in the new commodity produced, when he combines labour power with the material forms of capital he owns in the process of production. The surplus value acquired allows for the continuous (self-)expansion (or valorization) of capital even when all exchanges occur at 'full' values of the commodities involved. This was the fundamental conceptual advance made in Marx's enunciation of the labour theory of value.

[12] Marx, *Capital, Volume 1*, p. 49.

One consequence of these defining features of capitalism is that the circuit of capital relevant to the capitalist is the circuit of money and productive commodity capital. Money (M) as the ultimate expression of exchange value is deployed to acquire commodities in the form of means of production and labour power, to produce commodities that embody surplus value, which are then converted in the sphere of circulation to a larger sum of money (M'). The circuit M–C–M' is no more the result of accidental price variations or unequal exchange realized through the manipulations of merchant capitalists, but of the generation of the surplus value that allows for the constant self-expansion of value that is the form of existence of capital. This makes the production of use value incidental to (though necessary for) the capitalist who, as capital personified, is focused on the extraction of surplus value for accumulation. In so far as the capitalist is capital personified, 'his motivating force is not the acquisition and enjoyment of use-values, but the acquisition and augmentation of exchange-values. He is fanatically intent on the valorization of value; consequently he ruthlessly forces the human race to produce for production's sake.' In the process, however, he plays a progressive role and

> spurs on the development of society's productive forces, and the creation of those material conditions of production which alone can form the real basis of a higher form of society, a society in which the full and free development of every individual forms the ruling principle.[13]

It should be clear that what makes a commodity-produ-

---

[13] Marx, *Capital: A Critique of Political Economy* (*Das Kapital* series, Book 1), p. 739.

cing system quintessentially capitalist is not the universalization of exchange but the generalization of commodity production, in the sense that labour power too is a commodity. Unlike under slavery or feudalism where the slave owner or feudal lord controls the labourer, and has access to his or her labour time because of ownership, bondage and coercive power, the capitalist confronts the worker as the owner of labour power with the freedom to work for whomsoever she or he chooses. Since labour power is the capacity to labour, the labourer must also be in a position and willing to alienate this capacity and offer it for sale to the capitalist. For these choices to be made, she or he must be free in a double sense: free to dispose of her/his labour power as a commodity, and free of or separated from all commodities that would allow her/him to use and realize the value of her/his own capacity to labour.

Primitive Accumulation

Marx did, at times, present the realization of this dual freedom as the *first step* in the development of capitalism through a process of 'so-called' *primitive accumulation*, in which peasants and petty producers are separated through expropriation from possession, control or ownership of the means of production. Such expropriation was defended by bourgeois political economy as being the result of the accumulation of wealth by an elite that was 'diligent, intelligent and above all frugal'. However, in actual history it was, as Marx documented, the result of 'conquest, enslavement, robbery, murder, in short, force', that divorced producers from the means of production.[14] While 'emancipating' these producers from

---

[14] Ibid., p. 873.

serfdom and the fetters of guilds, it also left them with nothing to sell but their labour power.

There were also other forms in which non-market processes were used to accumulate capital as part of the processes of primitive accumulation.

> The rising bourgeoisie needs the power of the state, and uses it to 'regulate' wages, i.e. to force them into the limits suitable for making a profit, to lengthen the working day, and to keep the worker himself at his normal level of dependence. This is an essential part of so-called primitive accumulation.[15]

In fact, at the end of the seventeenth century in England, it took the form of a combination of moments that 'embraces the colonies, the national debt, the modern tax system, and the system of protection'.[16] Once this 'first step' was complete, capital accumulated at one pole confronts the doubly free worker, and capital accumulation based on surplus value extraction in production proceeds.

Accompanying and following this process is another transition that Marx presented as reflective of the development of capitalism proper. Since the magnitude of surplus value depends on the total length of the working day and the value of labour power, it can be increased either by lengthening the working day (*absolute surplus value*) or by reducing the value of labour power (*relative surplus value*), through productivity increases in the sectors producing the goods entering the worker's subsistence consumption basket.[17] In either case,

---

[15] Ibid., pp. 899–900.

[16] Ibid., p. 915.

[17] The aim of the productivity increase is not to shorten the working day of the labourer, but to shorten the necessary labour time in a given

since the ratio of surplus value to variable capital (or capital outlaid to cover the value of labour power) rises, so does the 'rate of exploitation', s/v, or the ratio of surplus labour to necessary labour or the value of labour power expended. But, in Marx's view, it was the extraction of relative surplus value through productivity-enhancing investments that was characteristic of capitalism in its fully developed form.

Since capital must confront 'doubly free' labour in the market for capital accumulation to occur in its full-fledged form, the fact that labour power in that form must emerge through a process of primitive accumulation affects the ability of the system to extract relative surplus value. When money capital first seeks to realize the circuit M–C–M', it does not have enough 'doubly free' workers ready at hand. It extracts surplus by bringing under its sway the existing world of peasants and petty producers operating with pre-existing techniques of production, or through what Marx identifies as the 'formal subsumption of labour to capital'.[18] In those conditions, since the technical conditions of production are given, only absolute surplus value can be extracted.

It is only when workers who have nothing to sell but their labour power confront capital accumulated in the hands of a few, that the conditions whereby the owners of capital can transform the process of production and enhance surplus value extraction in the form of relative surplus value are created. This is the phase of real subsumption of labour by

---

or even expanded working day. An increase in surplus value due to a change of this kind in the lengths of the two components of the working day amounts to an increase in relative surplus value.

[18] Marx, *Capital: A Critique of Political Economy* (*Das Kapital* series, Book 1), p. 645.

capital.[19] Here again, at many points in his analysis, Marx appears to suggest that the extraction of relative surplus value based on the real subsumption of labour by capital inevitably displaces the extraction of absolute surplus value through the formal subsumption of labour by capital. In Marx's view, the production of surplus value 'requires a specifically capitalist mode of production, a mode of production which, along with its methods, means and conditions, arises and develops spontaneously on the basis of the formal subsumption of labour under capital. This formal subsumption is then *replaced* by a real subsumption' (emphasis added).[20]

These suggestions – that primitive accumulation is only a first step in capitalist evolution and that absolute surplus value extraction will be displaced by relative surplus value extraction – could be interpreted as resulting from Marx's reading of the dynamism that post-industrial revolution capitalism displayed. It could also be seen as reflective of the view that a combination of workers' movements and legislation, in the form of the Factory Acts they led to in England, would force capital to limit the working day and to accelerate technical change such that accumulation depends largely on relative surplus value. These features, even then, were of course typical only of the empirical ground for Marx's analysis of capitalism.

As Marx noted in his Preface to the first German edition of *Capital*, his intention was to examine the capitalist mode of production, and the conditions of production and

---

[19] 'The production of absolute surplus value turns exclusively on the length of the working day, whereas the production of relative surplus value completely revolutionizes the technical processes of labour and the groupings into which society is divided.' Ibid., pp. 644–45.
[20] Ibid.

exchange corresponding to that mode, by analysing capitalism in England of that time, which was its 'classic ground'. The fact that other countries, including Germany, were not characterized by the dynamism that England displayed did not undermine the generality of that analysis, because: 'The country that is more developed industrially only shows, to the less developed, the image of its own future.'[21] In Marx's understanding, though by the time *Capital*, Volume 1 was completed, more than a century had passed since the emergence of industrial capitalism in England and elsewhere, the capitalist mode was not present in its pure form even in Germany where the first edition was launched. In practice, in most contexts including Germany, 'alongside of modern evils (of capitalism), a whole series of inherited evils' oppressed the people.

The Progressive Character of Capitalism

This primacy of the English case, with emphasis on its most progressive features, mattered in two ways for Marx's assessment of capitalism during the years he worked on *Capital*. First, the technological achievements of the industrial revolution in England made him conclude that while in time capitalist relations would prove a fetter on the productive forces, capitalism was a system that he saw, even in his more cynical writings, as having contributed to 'a wondrous development of the social productive forces'.[22] Second, Marx saw in this progressive character of capitalism an ability to ensure in

---

[21] Ibid., p. 91.
[22] Karl Marx, Draft 2 of letter to Vera Zasulich, quoted in Jones, *Karl Marx: Greatness and Illusion*, p. 583.

time, and perhaps inexorably, the displacement and demise of primitive methods of production and backward relations of production.

This kind of reading of the nature of actually existing capitalism was also encouraged by the fact that in *Capital* as it came to be published, Marx neither undertook an extensive analysis of the role of the state in supporting capitalist accumulation, and providing a site for the *persisting* primitive accumulation of capital; nor did he analyse the impact that capitalist expansion had on the peripheral countries and the colonies, where its 'modernizing' influence did not exclude coercive extraction of surplus, subordination of producers operating with primitive techniques, and reproduction of backward relations of production so as to maximize the extraction of absolute surplus value.

The resulting optimism about the transformative potential of capitalism and the increasing assertion of the collective will of the working class possibly explains the fact that Marx: (i) considered primitive accumulation to be confined to the early stages of capitalism, before the capital–wage labour relation is 'universalized' to a substantial extent; (ii) saw a sequential movement away from the formal to the real subsumption of labour by capital, and from the extraction of absolute surplus value to the extraction of relative surplus value; and (iii) argued that this transition would be hastened by the ability of the working class to both limit the length of the working day and raise the level of wages.

Actually Existing Capitalism

Any reading of world history over the last 150 years would indicate that the first two of the three features mentioned above have not been confined to specific phases of capitalism, but have persisted to differing degrees in different contexts across the history of capitalism. Even to the extent that Marx's analysis was true of the 'classic ground' of capitalism he analysed, namely England, it was by no means overwhelmingly the rule. And even though the expectation that capitalism would not survive through the nineteenth century or the first part of the twentieth century has been belied, the persistence of capitalism has not been accompanied by a transformation in which an end to primitive accumulation, a shift away from absolute surplus value extraction to relative surplus value extraction, and a strengthening of the power of collective labour to win concessions from capital, have been unambiguously visible. In what follows I argue that this persistence, in historically modified forms of primitive accumulation and the extraction of absolute surplus value (alongside relative surplus value resulting from the real subsumption of labour by capital), is a feature that is not just empirically observed, but is also crucial to an understanding of different phases of accumulation under actually existing capitalism. Applying these categories from Marx to an understanding of recent history enriches our understanding of the behaviour of capital in the Age of Finance.

Indeed, Marx too recognized that capital, focused on maximizing the enhancement of surplus value and accelerating capital accumulation, would continue to seek ways of extracting absolute surplus value, and that the workers' effort to limit that may be only partially successful. As his detailed discussion on the failure of the Factory Acts, the constant struggle to limit the working day, the tendency to increase the intensity of work within a given working day, and the resort to payment of time- and piece-wages makes clear, capital constantly aims to maximize surplus value through 'primitive' means. So, while a 'merely formal subsumption of labour under capital[23] suffices for the production of absolute surplus value' when needed, the 'unrestricted prolongation of the working day turned out to be a very characteristic product of large scale industry' even long after relative surplus value extraction had begun. In sum, it is completely possible that the generation of absolute and relative surplus value go hand in hand throughout the capitalist epoch and independent of the level of capitalist development.

This also occurs by ensuring that the worker is not paid the 'full' value of his labour power, as happens under the assumption that all commodities including labour power are exchanged as 'equivalents'. Since wages are paid in money, and take various forms such as time- and piece-wages, it is possible to reduce the wage per unit of time (say, an hour) to a level where the commodities the wage can buy are not enough to replenish the capacity to labour, and workers are forced to work long hours or more intensively in order even to earn a miserable wage. If surplus value is enhanced by paying workers less than the full value of their labour power, it is expanded through the expropriation of a part of what is the workers' due in any given social and historical context.

This remains true even 150 years after the publication of Marx's *Capital*. The growing presence of casual, temporary and self-employed workers, and the unleashing of competition between the reserve army of cheap labour constantly

---

[23] Or 'that handicraftsmen who previously worked on their own account, or as apprentices of a master, should become wage workers under the direct control of the capitalist'. Marx, *Capital: A Critique of Political Economy* (*Das Kapital* series, Book 1), p. 645.

reproduced in the peripheral countries and workers in the metropolitan centres, only aggravate this. These create conditions in which workers are forced to exploit themselves, creating opportunities for the extraction of absolute surplus value, even when technological advance helps enhance relative surplus value. Moreover, inasmuch as these conditions and the proliferation of finance result in indebtedness that leads to the loss of ownership or control over assets on the part of workers, the middle classes and the peasantry, the expropriation of assets that can be sold or used later in surplus value-generating productive activity becomes the means to extract surplus without the mediation of productive activity in the first instance.

Finally, any study of actually existing capitalism must treat it as a world system, and not just an English phenomenon. Marx's discussion of imperialism outside of *Capital*, in his *New York Tribune* articles, for example,[24] did recognize: (i) the role of surplus transfer and market access in the colonies in sustaining capital accumulation in the classic ground of capitalism, well past its early history; and (ii) the role of the subordination of the petty peasantry and capture of the state by capital in extracting the surplus that was transferred. Such transfers and market invasion continued to play a role through the twentieth century, and does so even today – now under the aegis of finance as well. So, the transformation that Marx took for granted, though visible and significant, has not been taken to completion even in the developed capitalist world, and definitely not in the large underdeveloped or less developed periphery of capitalism.

It is clear that the period after the Second World War,

---

[24] See Iqbal Husain, ed., *Karl Marx on India*, New Delhi: Tulika Books, with Aligarh Historians Society, 2006.

when unemployment in the developed world was low and welfare state measures were in place, was an exception rather than the rule. A feature of contemporary capitalism is the large size of the so-called 'informal sector' and high proportion of 'informal employment' – with workers employed in precarious conditions, and earning low and stagnant wages. This is evident in the less developed countries where the informal economy accounts for between one-half and three-quarters of all non-agricultural employment, with poor employment conditions involving lack of protection when wages are not paid, compulsory overtime, lay-offs without notice or compensation, and the absence of benefits such as pension and insurance. But with unemployment in the developed countries soaring and remaining high after the 2008 crisis, descriptions of the labour market point to precarious conditions in that part of the world as well. This has affected the young in particular, who are experiencing long spells of joblessness, suffer from large exposure to temporary and precarious jobs, and are forced to accept reductions in working time.

So, the dominant conclusion that emerges from an analysis of the last 150 years is the persistence, in changed forms, of extremely intense exploitation of workers and petty producers, especially in the periphery, through 'primitive' forms of subsumption, continued reliance on forms of absolute surplus value extraction, and the realization of all this at the expense of weakened labour with help from the state. The intensity of these means of exploitation increases when the correlation of power favours capital, and 'society' does not restrain it even partially. Moreover, ever since the onset of the monopoly phase of capitalism in the quarter-century since *Capital, Volume I* was published, the role of the state as the means and site for primitive accumulation has increased hugely.

Among the reasons for the resilience of capitalism are its ability to find new avenues to extract surpluses using old means. Even in contexts where the tendency for the rate of profit to fall operates, it can be counteracted by raising the rate of surplus value through resort to primitive means of surplus extraction or the use of the state apparatus, as we shall discuss later. However, the fact that capitalism has proved to be more resilient than Marx and Engels expected is a call not for dropping the analysis underpinning Marx's *magnum opus*, but for taking forward the open-ended discussion in the still-incomplete *Capital*, and for creatively applying the method developed by Marx and Engels. Such creative application must take into account the changes in capitalism at the end of that prolonged history, and the implications this has for the nature of capitalism and its dynamics. By the 1840s, which was when Marx's engagement with political economy began, England, having experienced the rise to dominance of capitalism, was in the midst of the transformation wrought by the industrial revolution, and had already emerged as the world's leading imperial power. At the beginning of the nineteenth century the majority of that country's work force was engaged in agriculture and related sectors, and the non-agricultural sector had the characteristics of a handicraft economy. By the late nineteenth century, however, factory production had become common. According to the 1851 Census, 46 per cent of the work force was employed in the secondary sector. This was the 'classic ground' that provided the empirical basis on which Marx built his critique of the 'classical economists'.

In comparison, circumstances in the Age of Finance are vastly different. In today's United Kingdom (UK), industry and construction account for 21 per cent of total value added, and agriculture and related activities for less than 1 per cent.

The figures are similar for the United States of America (USA) and Germany. Services dominate economic activity clearly and by a wide margin. Within services, 'finance, insurance and real estate' account for 19 per cent of total value added in the UK and USA, and 15 per cent in Germany.[25] In the USA, the share of domestic corporate profits accruing to financial companies increased from 7.8 per cent in 1947 to 24.9 per cent in 2000, and stood at 28.4 per cent in 2016.[26] The proliferation of finance has meant that financial assets have become an important mode of acquiring wealth, and ownership of financial assets an important means of capital accumulation.

Associated with these features of the Age of Finance is the evidence that over long periods, not only are the wages of workers slow to rise or even stagnant, contributing to rising inequality when productivity rises, but also the fact underlying this tendency that increasingly, 'regular' work is the exception rather than a rule, with a growing role for self-employment and casual, short-term employment. To the extent that across a stagnant average wage, wage rates per hour of work vary, workers are required, if the market permits, to extend their number of hours of work to achieve some historically given target wage that allows for the reproduction of labour power. An important factor underlying this tendency is the internationalization of capitalist production and finance, through which the large reserve army of cheap labour in the less devel-

---

[25] Figures from *OECD Factbook: 2015–16*, available in OECD. Stat at http://stats.oecd.org/. Value added in the Information and Communication sector stood at 6 per cent in the UK and USA, and 5 per cent in Germany.

[26] Figures from Federal Reserve Bank of St. Louis, available at https://fred.stlouisfed.org/tags/series?t=bea%3Bcorporate+profits.

oped countries is used as a weapon to tame the demands of workers in the developed countries for decent working conditions and a decent wage. In a fragmented and segmented labour market, the role of capital in this form of extraction of absolute surplus value may be missed. But these features of contemporary capitalism must influence any analysis of capitalism deriving directly from Marx's *Capital*, written while examining England's more dynamic industrial capitalism. How that possibly can be done is the dominant concern of this series of lectures.

2

Order and Anarchy in Capitalist Systems

When we return to *Capital* 150 years after the publication of the first edition of Volume 1, we do so with objectives that are contrary. Capitalism, though challenged by the Socialist revolutions in many countries of the world – starting with the October Revolution in Russia in 1917 and continuing through the establishment of the People's Republic of China in 1949 – has survived those challenges and is clearly dominant today. So, we partly seek to understand the resilience of capitalism, despite Marx's own understanding that the period of his engagement with political economy, starting in the 1840s, was one in which the inexorable logic of capitalist development had brought it to a point where its transcendence was imminent. But we are also interested in understanding its persisting vulnerability, reflected in periodic crises – not least the global financial crisis of 2007–08, the great recession that followed and the chronic recession that persists to this day. For that purpose, Marx's extensive analysis of the nature and determinants of crises under capitalism provides an obvious point of departure.

It is for the latter reason that even those who declare themselves convinced of the irrelevance of Marx's analysis are forced to reckon with it, even in periods when political forces influenced by that analysis are weak or in retreat. Marx's assessment that capitalism is crisis-prone, and his analysis of the instability and vulnerability of capitalism as a system, are too close to the truth to ignore. Capitalism may still survive, but its evolution has been and remains scarred by violent disruptions in activity, establishing the validity of Marx's understanding that such crises were an immanent feature of the dynamics of capitalism.

But that analysis in *Capital* and Marx's other writings is by no means complete, and possibly cannot be. At one level of abstraction, Marx read from capitalism's structure and dynamic, a tendency for orderly behaviour. The tendency towards an appearance of order in capitalism was in the first instance inherent in its advanced division of labour, because

> all the different kinds of private labour (which are carried on independently of each other, and yet, as spontaneously developed branches of the social division of labour, are in a situation of all-round dependence on each other) are continuously being reduced to the quantitative proportions in which society requires them.[1]

If there is any divergence of the share of labour allotted to a particular sector from the requirement set by demand for the output it produces, output and prices diverge from their equilibrium values because of excess supply or excess demand in individual sectors.

[1] Karl Marx, *Capital: A Critique of Political Economy* (*Das Kapital* series, Book 1), Penguin Books, Kindle edition, 1976, p. 168.

Only so much of any commodity will be sold in total as there is social demand for it. So, through adjustments of prices, demand and supply, social labour time gets reallocated across commodities so as to ensure that demand and supply match, and production is in line with what is socially necessary. Thus, 'in the midst of the accidental and ever-fluctuating exchange relations between the products, the labour time necessary to produce them asserts itself as a regulative law of nature'.[2] The process need not be immediate or smooth but the tendency is for the system to restore order and balance, even if that is achieved at the cost of wasted or unutilized resources and unemployed labour. This, then, is the law of value as it operates at the social level, independent of the will and actions of independent operators.'The owners of commodities find that the same social division of labour which turns them into independent private producers also makes the social process of production and the relations of the individual producers to each other within that process independent of the producers themselves.'[3]

This tendency to order notwithstanding, in any system of widespread commodity production, disruption of the circuit of commodities is likely. This is because of the presence of money. For example, a disruption can occur if circumstances encourage individual transactors to exploit the fact that money as the universal equivalent can be held without transacting, simply as a store of value. Marx argued that with the emergence of a money commodity as the universal equivalent, Say's Law, which states that supply creates its own demand, does not hold. To quote: 'Nothing could be more

[2] Ibid.
[3] Ibid., pp. 201–02.

foolish than the dogma that because every sale is a purchase, and every purchase a sale, the circulation of commodities necessarily implies an equilibrium between sales and purchases.'[4] While sale and purchase constitute a single identical act when occurring between two persons, when performed by the same person they are two distinct acts separated in time and space. 'No one can sell unless someone purchases. But no one directly needs to purchase because he has just sold.'[5] If he or she does not, the circuit is broken, preventing the 'realization' of the value concealed in commodities. That disruption will affect the demand for and/or supply of other commodities, and the 'crisis' spreads from its point of origin.

Antagonism and Anarchy in the Circuit of Money Capital

This, however, is a description of the circuit of commodities, whereas under capitalism proper what matters is the circuit of money capital, aimed at enhancing value. And given the antagonistic nature of capitalism, the 'anarchy' that characterizes it and the contradictory tendencies these generate, there are even more reasons why capitalist evolution can never be smooth. Capitalism is antagonistic because of the nature of the relation between capital and wage labour, and profits and wages. It is anarchic not because the system is in a permanent state of disarray, which it is not, but because it is inevitable that in a system with private property, the investment decisions that drive accumulation are made by competing, atomistic producers in uncoordinated fashion.

The antagonistic character of the capitalist mode is

[4] Ibid., p. 208.
[5] Ibid.

reflected in a constant effort by capital to increase, at the expense of wages, the share of surplus value that can be appropriated. Capitalist production is aimed not at delivering use values but at producing ever-increasing exchange values through the extraction of surplus value. This affects the 'laws of motion' of capitalism that unfold by making individual capitalists behave as capital personified, nothing more than 'cogs in the wheels' of a larger mechanism geared to the continuous self-enhancement of value.

The drive to enhance surplus value implies a persisting tendency to hold down wages and even depress them, which adversely affects the consumption of workers. On the other hand, capitalists do not consume all the surplus that accrues to them, but are forced to allocate a large and rising proportion of it for accumulation. This constantly enlarges the mass of commodities brought to the market for sale. The resulting competition between capitals to win for themselves an adequate share of the market to realize surplus value operates as an 'external coercive law'. It forces capitalists to constantly adopt new methods of production that replace workers with machines, reducing the number of workers and the outlays on variable capital, while increasing the mass of constant capital and (possibly) the volume of constant capital in terms of value. This gives rise to the following contradiction: capital is driven to expand production, but simultaneously constrains demand by depressing wages, increasing the unemployed work force and limiting capitalists' consumption. This creates a potential source of disproportionality between the capacity of the system to produce goods and services, and the demand for them, leading to a crisis of overproduction or underconsumption.

On more than one occasion Marx pointed to this contradiction between the need for expansion under capitalism, and the restriction of consumption that results from the drive to limit the wages of workers (or necessary labour) and raise surplus value, on the one hand, and curb capitalist consumption to maximize accumulation, on the other. In a footnote in Volume 2 of *Capital* Marx notes: 'The workers are important for the market as buyers of commodities. But as sellers of their commodity – labour-power – capitalist society has the tendency to restrict them to their minimum price.'[6] Further,

> the periods in which capitalist production exerts all its forces regularly show themselves to be periods of over-production; because the limit to the application of the productive powers is not simply the production of value, but also its realization. However, the sale of commodities, the realization of commodity capital, and thus of surplus-value as well, is restricted not by the consumer needs of society in general, but by the consumer needs of a society in which the great majority are always poor and must always remain poor.[7]

However, where wages and the length of the working day settle is determined not just by the needs of capitalist accumulation, but the state of play in the class struggle. If unemployment is low and worker resistance strong, holding down wages or lengthening the working day is not easy or assured. Rapid accumulation by increasing the demand for labour at a faster rate than the growth of the labour force reduces the level of unemployment and tends to raise wages. On the other hand, if wages rise and the length of the working day shrinks, so do profits, adversely affecting the pace of

---

[6] Karl Marx, *Capital, Volume 2* (*Das Kapital* series, Book 2), Chapter 16, fn 1: p. 599, Penguin Books, Kindle edition, 1978.
[7] Ibid.

accumulation and threatening slow growth or stagnation. There are indeed phases in capitalist history, some discussed by Marx in *Capital*, when a shortage of labour tends to raise wages and squeeze profits. Given the antagonistic nature of the capital–labour relation and the drive of capitalists to shore up profits, the capitalist response is to reduce dependence on living labour by substituting it with dead labour in the form of more advanced and productive means of production.

So, the tendency to adopt more productive labour-displacing machinery that is unleashed by the competition between capitals is now intensified by the need to reduce dependence on living labour. The result is that the demand for labour can fall short of that necessary to absorb even those newly entering the labour force, leave alone absorb the backlog of the unemployed. In the event, an abiding feature of capitalism is an unemployed reserve army of labour that is replenished every time its contraction raises wages and threatens profits. Capitalism needs the pressure exerted by a large relative surplus population, by a large reserve army of labour, on the level of worker resistance, to render wages downward-flexible and the working day elastic. This need for a reserve army to discipline workers and keep wages under control gives the constant process of technical change driven by the competition between capitals an independent justification within the logic of the system. But it can also aggravate the disproportionality between the capacity of the system to produce and the consumption it stimulates, leading to crises of overproduction. This is one more way in which the antagonistic nature of capitalism sets up a tendency for the system to experience a crisis.

Along with being antagonistic, capitalism, as noted, is a system that is 'anarchic' because of uncoordinated decision-making. This too makes the system crisis-prone. As Marx repeatedly stressed, capitalist production is production meant for sale that allows not merely for the reflux of the value advanced by the capitalist in the form of constant and variable capital, but also for the realization of the surplus value embedded in capitalist produce. If the latter does not happen, the essence of capitalism, the completion of the circuit M–C–M', is challenged. For the value of commodities produced in any period to be realized, demand for the same must exist. But whether this demand exists or not depends on aggregate demand in the system and its composition, which in turn depends on the aggregate investment made by all capitalists and the income it generates. Since no single capitalist knows what other capitalists plan to do in terms of the volume and area of investment they would choose, and must rely on guesstimates of what the others are likely to do, there is no reason why the expectations of each and all of them regarding the demand for their output should be realized. Excess production in some areas and shortages in others are inevitable, necessitating *ex-post* adjustments in production capacity to restore an equilibrium. The process involves painful adjustments in the form of unemployment, bankruptcy and waste of resources.[8]

Thus, despite the sense of order conveyed by the law of value and by Marx's reading of the 'laws of motion' of capitalism, the antagonism and anarchy characteristic of capitalism inevitably burst forth in violent eruptions. While Marx refers to many routes through which this could occur, there is no single, complete or overarching theory of crisis in Marx: the unfinished work in *Capital* and elsewhere provides us only the

[8] Maurice Dobb, *An Essay on Economic Growth and Planning*, London: Routledge, Kegan and Paul, 1960.

apparatus with which we can approach analysis of any particular crisis. What we have are different tendencies – driven by the logic of capitalist development, and triggered by specific, occasionally fortuitous circumstances – that can precipitate a crisis. And then again they may not, if they are held back by counteracting tendencies that weaken or neutralize the crisis-generating ones. As Marx noted in *Theories of Surplus Value*, 'the real crisis can be explained only from the real movement of capitalist production, competition and credit',[9] since that real context is far more complex than an abstract discussion of the self-expansion of value in a world of capitalist commodity production geared to extract surplus value.

Law of the Tendency of the Rate of Profit to Fall

However, partly because Marx did spend much time elaborating one particular explanation for crisis, and partly perhaps because of the way in which his notes were put together for the later volumes of *Capital*, a view gained ground that one explanation of crisis, which can lead to chronic depression as capitalism matures, held a privileged position in Marx's analysis. This was the 'law of the tendency of the rate of profit to fall', where, to recall, the rate of profit is defined as the ratio of surplus value to total capital, or the sum of constant and variable capital outlaid by the capitalist.[10] The drive to accu-

---

[9] Karl Marx, *Theories of Surplus Value*, II: 2, Moscow: Progress Publishers, n.d., p. 286.

[10] When referring to the rate of profit, it is necessary to point to the implications of inevitable variations in the organic composition of capital (or the ratio of constant to variable capital, c/v) across sectors at any given point in time, because of the different technical characteristics of different industries. While the rate of exploitation of

mulate on the part of independent and atomistic producers, as well as the pressure to invest in new methods of production that reproduce the reserve army of labourers, had, according to Marx, one important implication: a rise in the ratio of constant to variable capital used in production, or the 'organic composition of capital'. Since the rate of profit is calculated as $s/(c+v)$, it can be expressed as a ratio in which the rate of surplus value (s/v) features in the numerator, and the organic composition of capital (c/v) features in the denominator: $\{(s/v)/[(c/v)+1]\}$. So, for a given rate of exploitation, the rate of profit tends to fall as the organic composition of capital rises. If indeed there is a tendency for the organic composition of capital to rise as capitalism matures, the system would be faced with an inexorable decline in the rate of profit, which in turn would destroy the incentive to accumulate, pushing it into a phase of chronic slow growth, stagnation and even depression.

---

labour power is given by the ratio of surplus value to variable capital (s/v), what matters to an individual capitalist is the surplus earned on the total capital advanced, or $s/(c+v)$ or $\{(s/v)/(c/v)+1\}$, which is the rate of profit. So, even when the rate of surplus value (s/v) in two sectors is the same, rates of profit, which is what concerns the individual capitalist, can differ because of differences in (c/v). If that is the case, since money capital either as interest-bearing or dividend-seeking capital can and will flow to any sector where the rate of profit is higher, production in sectors offering higher profits would rise, driving down prices and equating the rates of profit.

This creates a difficulty if we assume, as Marx did, that the rate of surplus value is equated across sectors. If this were true but the organic composition of capital was to differ, the rate of profit would be different across the two sectors. This cannot be sustained, since the mobility of capital and the force of competition would work to do away with those differentials. If the sum of value is equal to the sum of prices, the total volume of profits cannot be equal to the total surplus value generated by the system. While conducting his initial analysis of capi-

However, as even Marx was quick to note, there are many counteracting tendencies that can weaken or negate this process. The most important of these is that, parallel to the rise in the organic composition of capital, the rate of surplus value may rise as capitalists compensate for the effect of a rising (c/v) by increasing the rate of surplus value (s/v). This they can do by lengthening the working day, or increasing the intensity of labour, or depressing real wages below their value. All of these are possible and have been observed even in later stages of capitalism's development. But more importantly, the reason why capitalists choose to introduce new methods of production, potentially raising the organic composition of capital, is the need to increase the extraction of relative surplus value through productivity increases. Hence, we cannot assume that the rate of surplus value remains constant when the organic composition of capital rises. On the other hand, a rise in the

---

talism by assuming that organic compositions of capital, and therefore rates of surplus value and rates of profit, are simultaneously equal across sectors in Volume 3 of *Capital*, Marx dropped the assumption of equality of organic compositions. Needless to say, this resulted in a divergence of prices of production from values, to discuss which Marx devoted a whole section. Unfortunately, the discussion could not arrive at a fully satisfactory explanation of the relation between the two.

The differences in organic competition of capital dilute the determining influence of the law of value as defined by the labour time-based values of commodities. Two questions arise. The first is whether there is any solution to this so-called 'transformation problem', of transforming values into prices of production, or establishing a formal link between the latter and the former. The second is whether dilution of the determining influence of the law of value is a reason to drop the labour theory of value itself. The answer to the first question is 'yes'; many forms of the solution are available, which I do not plan to go into here. But the second question bears discussion. To start

rate of surplus value can counteract the tendency for the rate
of profit to fall. Hence, there is no reason to expect the 'law'
of the falling rate to apply as a normal or dominant tendency.

Another tendency counteracting the falling rate of profit
could be productivity improvements in industries producing and supplying constant capital, which may prevent the
value of constant capital from increasing at the same rate as its
material volume, or even keep the rate of increase in the value
of constant capital below that for variable capital, so that c/v
in fact falls. If that be the case, even if the technical composition of capital shifts in favour of constant capital, the organic
composition need not, thereby countering the tendency for
the rate of profit to fall.

However, it is completely possible that the rate of profit
in certain phases of capitalism falls for reasons other than a
rise in the organic composition of capital. In particular, as
noted earlier, rapid accumulation could result in a depletion
of the reserve army of labour, raising wages above their values
and squeezing profits. That is, the difficulty is not with the
idea that the rate of profit can fall below what capitalists consider 'normal' at any given point in time, and adversely affect
the pace of accumulation. The difficulty is with attributing

---

with, besides being a first step in any explanation of exchange values,
the fundamental objective and contributions of the labour theory of
value are to identify the source of surplus value (in the difference
between the value of labour power and the length of the working day)
and to develop a commodity theory of money in which the prices of
commodities are finally represented. Identifying the source of surplus
value is not just important in itself, but crucial, because the issue of
the redistribution of profits among capitalists to equate the rate of
profit across sectors can only follow if the source and determinants of
the volume of aggregate profits are identified.

the fall in the profit rate to a rise in the organic composition of capital in a context where the rate of surplus value remains constant or rises at a slower rate than the organic composition of capital.

Crises and the Disruption of Reproduction

Whatever be the cause of the crisis, what it does is to disrupt the process of reproduction under capitalism. The fact that the reproduction of the system can be disrupted in multiple ways was captured in Marx's discussion of the inter-sectoral balance requirements needed for such reproduction. His discussion of this issue begins with an examination of the prerequisites needed for a system to reproduce itself by producing the same output in terms of volume and composition, period after period, or for *simple reproduction* to occur.

In a simple framework of labour allocation across industries, the economy can be divided into two Departments, I and II, with Department I producing the means of production (consisting of instruments of production and objects of labour or constant capital) employed in both sectors, and Department II producing the consumption goods catering to both workers and capitalists. The value of output in each of these sectors would consist of the sum of the value of constant capital consumed in production (the means of production), the value of variable capital outlaid to pay workers their wages, and the surplus value yielded by the variable capital ($c+v+s$).

The minimum requirement for a viable capitalist system would be that it reproduces itself by ensuring that out of every year's production, at least as much output is made available from the two sectors as to replace the constant and variable capital consumed in that year, in the forms in which they enter production and consumption. That is, for the same level of output to be produced year after year, during each year, the instruments of production, objects of labour and means of consumption productively or non-productively absorbed must be replaced, assuming that the workers consume the whole of their wages and the capitalists all the surplus that accrues to them. This is simple reproduction of the system.

There is a collateral condition that is implicitly met for this to occur, assuming that the workers consume the whole of their wages and the capitalists consume the entire surplus that accrues to them. While in value terms, the sum of constant capital, variable capital and surplus defines the value of output in each sector, materially speaking, workers and capitalists in Department I cannot eat the means of production (called investment goods for simplicity) produced, and capitalists in Department II cannot deploy the consumption goods they produce for investment. During any production period, while the investment goods required in Department I can be met from its own output, the consumption of workers (v_1) and that of capitalists (s_1) must be met from the consumption goods produced in Department II. Conversely, in Department II, while the consumption of workers and capitalists can be met from the output of that Department, the requirement of investment goods must be met from the output of Department I. There is, therefore, demand for consumption goods and excess supply of means of production totalling $v_1 + s_1$ in Department I, and demand for constant capital and excess supply of means of consumption amounting to c_2 in Department II. This requires a steady exchange between the two Departments: the excess elements of constant capital (c_2) must flow from Department I to Department II to meet the reproduction needs of the latter, and the excess elements of consumption (of value $v_1 + s_1$) must flow from Department II to Department I to satisfy the consumption requirements of workers and capitalists located in the latter. For simple reproduction to be complete and stable, these flows must match: i.e. the variable capital and surplus components consumed in Department I must equal the constant capital requirement in Department II. This is the material balance requirement for uninterrupted simple reproduction. If this condition does not hold, there would be overproduction or an excess supply of goods produced in one or other of the Departments.

However, defining or delineating the requirements for material balance does not guarantee uninterrupted reproduction. In the production process, only the value equivalents of constant and variable capital and of surplus value are congealed in the commodities produced. Workers are paid wages in money and obtain the material equivalent of those wages not directly from capitalists in Department II but from the market. Similarly, capitalists in Department II must turn to the market to replenish their material capital, for which they need to sell commodities to accumulate the money capital needed to buy commodity capital. If, having sold commodities for money, one or more agents choose not to use that money to demand goods, demand for some goods will fall short of supply. Capital advanced by the producers of those goods cannot be recouped and advanced again as means of production or wages for labour. Reproduction cannot occur. Thus, developments in the sphere of circulation that result in any imbalance between supply and demand can disrupt reproduction.

Moreover, simple reproduction cannot be a capitalist form, since the motivating force of the capitalist, as argued, is not the acquisition and enjoyment of use values, but the acquisition and augmentation of exchange values. The capitalist 'is fanatically intent on the valorization (self-enhancement) of value'.[11] This implies that the capitalist system cannot just reproduce itself at a given level of output, but must ensure expanded reproduction. This must occur through the actions of each capitalist, who should not consume all the surplus but must invest a proportion, perhaps a greater proportion, of her/his surplus value. The expansion that follows, however, puts each capitalist in competition with another. To survive and grow, the capitalist must constantly garner a share of a growing market that facilitates an increase in the volume of her/his production. To be able to produce and sell a larger volume of value and output, he/she must therefore prevent other competing capitalists from displacing her/him in the market. Capitalists must, therefore, constantly innovate, or invest in new methods of production, to stay at or ahead of the average social labour needed to produce a unit of any commodity required to remain competitive.

The implications of expanded reproduction can be illustrated by continuing with our example of two sectors and retaining the assumption that the workers consume all of their wages. The capitalists, on the other hand, must now consume only a part of the surplus value they extract, and advance the remaining partly in the form of constant capital and partly as variable capital, so as to expand operations. So, unlike in the case of simple reproduction, the output in both Departments I and II must be more than needed to just replace the investment goods and consumption goods consumed in that year. Now, the output must be large enough to deploy additional constant capital and combine that capital with a larger

---

[11] Marx, *Capital: A Critique of Political Economy* (*Das Kapital* series, Book 1), p. 739.

advance to employ additional workers, whose consumption needs have to be provided for. In this case, the larger volume of investment goods required in Department II must be bought in exchange for the larger volume of consumption goods needed to match the demands from the higher aggregate wage bill paid in Department I to hire a larger number of workers as well as any increase in consumption out of the surplus of the capitalists. In other words, the enhanced sum of variable capital and consumed surplus value in Department I must equal the enhanced requirements of constant capital supplied by Department I to Department II.

The implication of this balancing condition is that if the surplus value that is used each year to invest in constant capital and variable capital so as increase production and augment value is not distributed across industries and departments in the appropriate proportion, surpluses and shortages would ensue. This is likely in a context where the decision of what capacities to expand are taken by independent decision-makers who only have guesstimates of what other capitalists are likely to do, which would influence the supplies offered by the latter and the demand for the products of the former. Under the capitalist division of labour, independent producers engage in the production of separate commodities in the belief that there is demand for their products that can convert the value embedded in them into money form. This money will in turn allow the producers concerned to acquire other commodities from similarly placed producers to meet their needs for productive or individual consumption. If there is no investment coordination, the likelihood is low that an appropriate division of investment and additional capacity needed for balance will be realized. This provides the basis for realization crises resulting from disproportionality between departments.

Underconsumption as a Disproportionality

Underlying this disproportionality can be faster growth of Department I relative to Department II, or disproportionality between the rates of growth of the departments producing means of production and the means of consumption. But when such disproportionality leads to a situation where the growth in demand for consumption goods is lower than the supply resulting from the process of accumulation, instability and crises are the result. Such crises of overproduction or underconsumption are also forms of disproportionality crises.[12]

Tugan-Baranowski argued that there was no reason why this should occur under capitalism, because it is possible to lay out the reproduction schemes such that despite a small consumption goods sector, the production of machines to produce machines to produce consumption goods more productively can ensure that the criteria for balance across sectors are achieved.[13] The demand for consumption goods from Department I is relatively small, and so is the demand for capital goods from Department II. Growth occurs primarily through additional production of machines used in Department I itself. Capitalism does not produce for consumption but for profit, so this, it can be argued, is also logically plausible. However, delineating the possibility of a balance with a large Department I and a small or miniscule Department II does not explain how this kind of balance will

---

[12] Paul M. Sweezy, *The Theory of Capitalist Development*, London: Dennis Dobson, 1946.

[13] Michal Kalecki, 'The problem of effective demand with Tugan-Baranowski and Rosa Luxemburg', in *Selected Essays on the Dynamics of the Capitalist Economy*, Cambridge: Cambridge University Press, 1971.

be realized under capitalism. Moreover, capitalists too invest because they are 'induced' by a market they hope to cater to, and for Department I capitalists, an important market is not one in which they produce for each other but one that caters to production of consumption goods. If, through some form of investment coordination, a structure of producing machines to produce machines can be organized, then, with even stagnant or declining consumption it would be possible to realize surplus value in an expanding system that also sees a rise in the aggregate volume of constant capital relative to variable capital. Workers may be left unemployed, but inter-sectoral balance conditions can hold and the system can keep growing. However, the problem in capitalism is that no such coordination is possible. Private property and competition between capitals renders it impossible. Oligopoly or even monopoly, while changing the nature of competition of capitals, can in fact intensify it. Further, if a government is to intervene to manage the competition adequately to ensure investment coordination, it must abolish the atomism inherent in a system with private property, or ensure the transcendence of capitalism. And in environments where coordination is possible, social objectives will drive that coordination, and consumption will be an important target of social production.

Marx's Theory and Actual Crises

Embedded in these discussions in *Capital* was the idea that the structural characteristics of the capitalist mode and certain tendencies that were inherent to the process of capitalist accumulation rendered the system unstable and prone to crises. While this idea was developed based on Marx's study of capitalist history till the time of writing of Volume I, the subsequent history of capitalism has only established how prescient he was. The anarchy of capitalism, as Marx described it, led to the Great Depression despite the access to colonial markets that many advanced capitalist countries had. In the event, the much-celebrated 'Keynesian revolution' concluded that it was inherent in the nature of capitalism that investment levels and the volume of aggregate demand needed to employ the available labour force in full were unlikely to be normally realized. So, a proactive state must intervene and invest when the 'animal spirits' of capitalists fail to deliver investment and output levels corresponding to full employment. This formed the basis for the 'welfare state' established in the aftermath of the Second World War in the United States of America and other advanced capitalist nations, during what came to be known as the Golden Age – of sustained growth and low employment. At that time, the argument gained ground that informed governments had found ways to address the weaknesses of capitalism, making capitalist cycles and recessions, leave alone depressions, a part of history.

However, this exceptional episode in the history of capitalism exacerbated rather than resolved the antagonism typical of capitalism that Marx had underlined in *Capital*. With sustained capitalist expansion, the demand for labour in the advanced nations pushed them closer to near-full employment, and their demand for primary commodities imported from the periphery rose. The result was a rise in wages, on the one hand, and in energy and raw material costs, on the other. The fall-out was partly inflation and partly a profits squeeze, which triggered a new crisis in global capitalism. What followed was a backlash against the welfare state that led to its unravelling through forms of capitalist restructuring that weakened the working class in advanced capitalist countries, limited its power, and prepared the ground for a restoration of the hegemony of big capital at the expense of workers and petty producers. In that process, new forms of exploitation of the periphery of global capitalism, through the relocation of manufacturing, came in handy.

What was crucial to this capitalist 'success' was that the crises that capitalism experienced did not serve as circumstances for the transcendence of the system itself. Despite the failed revolutions of 1848 and the failure of the 1857–58 crisis to generate the revolutionary ferment that Marx and Engels expected it to have, the idea that crises in capitalism would garner support for political movements aimed at overthrowing the system was central to their understanding. As late as 1873, in his 'Afterword to the Second Edition' of Volume 1 of *Capital,* Marx noted:

> The contradictory movement of capitalist society impresses itself upon the practical bourgeois most strikingly in the changes of the periodic cycle through which modern industry runs and whose crowning point is the general crisis. The crisis is once again approaching, although as yet but in its preliminary stage, and by the universality of its theatre and the intensity of its action it will drum dialectics even into the heads of the mushroom upstarts of the new, holy Prusso-German empire.[14]

Here too one can discern a sense of living in revolutionary times, even if not at a revolutionary moment. And one reason for this was the belief that the loss of legitimacy that capitalism would suffer because of a 'general' crisis and the pain that crisis would inflict on the working class would galvanize

[14] Karl Marx, *Capital, Volume 1*, Moscow: Progress Publishers, 1974, p. 29 (German edition 1873).

the latter into recognizing its role and move to overthrow the system. But this political requirement for the transcendence of capitalism was crucial, since being prone to crises did not mean that capitalism as an economic mechanism would break down and collapse.

In the period when Marx was engaged in writing *Capital*, at least two such eruptions – that occurred in 1847–48 and 1857–58 – were the focus of his attention, and perhaps influenced his notion of the 'decennial cycle' which he referred to more than once. But if the issue is one of cycles, are we arguing that a crisis when it occurs is self-correcting? To an extent, yes. One consequence of the depression is the underutilization or destruction of capital in some areas, and deflation in the value of capital assets in others. On the other hand, unemployment swells the ranks of the reserve army of labour, driving wages down below its value. Developments such as these revive profits and encourage investment that lead to a recovery. Thus, crisis is also a means of restructuring capital so as to restore balance and reinstate the collapsed process of accumulation. To the extent it is that, the theory of crisis deriving from such developments is also a theory of business cycles, which Marx identified as a decennial cycle in capitalism: a cycle that through its 'periods of average activity, production at high pressure, crisis and stagnation, depends on the constant formation, the greater or less absorption, and the re-formation of the industrial reserve army of surplus population'.[15]

But the possibility that recovery from a crisis can occur because of developments precipitated by the crisis itself does not imply that this is always necessarily true. Deflation in asset values can affect the confidence of capital so much that

---

[15] Marx, *Capital, Volume 2* (*Das Kapital* series, Book 2), p. 785.

the system is trapped in chronic depression. Capitalism does not break down for economic reasons, but chronic depression for long periods is quite possible and has been observed in practice. But in such instances too, if political developments which ensure that capitalism is transcended do not successfully unfold, capital will seek out ways to restore profits and accumulation. This would include reliance on features of capitalism that, as I earlier argued, Marx, in his search for the source of surplus value in a world of exchange of equivalents and the laws of motion of capitalism in its classic ground, did not emphasize. These features include the continuing presence of forms of extraction of absolute surplus value, the persistence of forms of primitive accumulation, and the exploitation of precariously employed workers and petty producers, especially in the periphery of global capitalism.

One obvious way in which capitalism finds its way out of a crisis is to transfer the burden of the crisis on to workers and petty producers, especially in the periphery, by adopting means of extracting more 'absolute surplus value', in the absence of the incentive to invest in new methods to increase relative surplus value.[16] This can also entail transferring some of the burden on to social reproduction, which involves unpaid labour within families and communities, which contributes to but is still 'outside' the capitalist system *per se*. The other is to resort to exports to markets in peripheral econo-

---

[16] For a conceptual elaboration of the role this plays in a theory of imperialism and in the stability of capitalism, see Utsa Patnaik and Prabhat Patnaik, *A Theory of Imperialism*, New York: Columbia University Press and New Delhi: Tulika Books, 2016; and Prabhat Patnaik, *Accumulation and Stability under Capitalism*, Oxford: Clarendon Press, 1997.

mies and to extract surpluses from these economies through colonial expansion or neo-colonial exploitation. The role that pre-capitalist sectors play here, in the expansion of capitalism, by providing it with sources of surplus and external markets, has been crucial throughout its history. This was done through coercive means that displaced and eliminated indigenous populations, appropriated land and resources, imported slaves and indentured labourers to work that land and exploit those resources, expropriated produce for export to the metropolis and opened up markets for metropolitan products. Rosa Luxemburg's argument[17] of the impossibility of a closed capitalist system, interpreted as an emphasis on the role of and the importance of non-capitalist markets as a source of inducements to invest, underlines this and was perhaps not always fully understood.[18]

Domestically, the means to address crises was to use the state as a means to generate demand, with state expenditure serving as an 'external' stimulus for capitalist growth till as long as it could be undertaken and financed in sustainable ways. This, as discussed, was successfully experimented with through the New Deal in the USA in the aftermath of the Great Depression, and, more significantly, during the post-war Golden Age, when public expenditure by the welfare state served as an automatic stabilizer, giving rise to the view that capitalism had rid itself of crises. A less benign version of this role of the state was, of course, the military–industrial complex, which was capitalism's aggressive effort to keep deep crises at bay. It was when such state expenditure could not be

---

[17] Rosa Luxemburg, *Accumulation of Capital* [1913], London: Routledge and Kegan Paul, 1951.
[18] Patnaik, *Accumulation and Stability under Capitalism*, pp. 22–28.

sustained without spurring inflation that capitalism's Golden Age came to an end.

As noted in the first lecture, since his larger project of writing a six-book version of *Capital*, as indicated in the Preface to *A Contribution to the Critique of Political Economy* (covering capital, landed property, wage labour, the state, foreign trade, the world market) could not be executed, Marx did not spend adequate time analysing the role of the last three in reducing the vulnerability of capitalism in its metropolitan centres. These factors undoubtedly had a role in explaining the fact that the material challenge to capitalism arose in the periphery, starting with the Socialist revolution in the Soviet Union, and the antagonism inherent in the system has not as yet led to its transcendence in the metropolitan core. In which case, that would explain the resilience of capitalism as well. But what is clear is that the resilience, if induced by these forces, has not precluded the system from being subject to crises, which seem once again to be increasing in their periodicity, intensity and length.

The complex influences on the ideas of any age, and the political developments that accompany them, are doubtless important to an understanding of why capitalism survived these 150 years and exists even today. But having survived, capitalism had to find ways of restructuring itself. Following the tendency towards stagnation that began in the 1960s and gathered momentum in the 1970s, restructuring took a form in which finance capital acquired a more important role in the capitalist accumulation process, aided by deregulation. The most obvious way was by expanding credit: housing mortgages, automobile and consumer durable loans, credit card receivables, besides corporate credit – all of which contributed to increasing demand. The coming of securitization, which allowed for the transfer and sharing of risk, also facilitated an expansion of the universe of borrowers, enlarging further the market for all goods and their input producers. In addition, there was an amplifying effect on such demand that the operations of finance had. By generating a speculative boom in asset (housing and stock) markets, it delivered a 'wealth effect', making households feel richer than they were and encouraging consumption out of future incomes by borrowing today. This also had significant effects on the real economy, expanding demand and substituting debt-financed private consumption and investment for debt-financed public expenditure as a stimulus to growth. This form of restructuring has transformed capitalism hugely relative to the way it looked and functioned in Marx's time. But Marx did have many insights on the role of money, credit and finance that provide a point of departure for understanding the functioning of the new capitalism. In the next lecture we turn to those insights, and revisit *Capital* in the Age of Finance.

3

Reading Marx's *Capital*
in the Age of Finance

Since its inception, and over the last 150 years since the publication of Volume 1 of *Capital*, capitalism has not merely
experienced many crises of varying intensity, but has been
transformed in fundamental ways. Important phases through
which those transformations have taken the capitalist system
are, for example, the mercantilist, industrial and monopoly
phases, though as a world system capitalism has always combined versions of its many forms. In many instances, the
transformation was a result of the restructuring that capitalism went through in the wake of crises, often due to deliber-
ate efforts of the state. Thus, in the last 150 years, two crises
in particular have had important transformative effects on the
system: the Great Depression, and the crisis of the late 1960s
and after. The effects of the 2007–08 crisis are, of course, still
unfolding.

The Great Depression, the effects of which capitalism
finally overcame only during the Second World War, led to a
major restructuring of capitalism initiated by the New Deal,
with public expenditure driving growth, reducing unemploy-

ment and ensuring a degree of social security, while speculative finance was kept in control. But, as I had discussed in the previous lecture, the antagonistic and anarchic character of capitalism made this phase just that: exceptional. The unusual coincidence of relatively high growth, near-full employment and low inflation could not last, as inflation emerged as a problem and the government's response to it triggered stagnation.

Following the tendency towards stagflation that began in the 1960s and gathered momentum in the 1970s, the next phase of restructuring not only dismantled much that was put in place in the three decades after the mid-1930s, but also took a form in which finance capital acquired a more important role in the capitalist accumulation process. Inflation forced the United States (US) government to give up its policy of regulated and low interest rates, since negative real (inflation-adjusted) interest rates resulted in the exit of savings from the banking system, threatening a banking crisis. When interest rates were raised by banks competing with each other to attract deposits, they had to be permitted to invest in higher-return but more risky areas to match the increased cost of capital. Volatility in the financial markets increased, encouraging hedging of risk with new instruments.

An era of large-scale securitization began, involving the creation of derivatives backed by financial assets of various kinds. Financial managers, using the freedom to innovate provided by deregulation, were soon 'manufacturing' innovative products that they created and sold in return for lucrative incomes in the form of fees and commissions. Since securitization allowed for the transfer and sharing of risk, not only did the size of the financial sector increase hugely, so did the overhang of financial products and the volume of risk in the system. There was an expansion, in tandem, of the universe of borrowers, many of sub-prime quality, whose debt-financed spending enlarged the market for all goods and their input producers. This had significant effects on the real economy, expanding demand and substituting debt-financed private consumption for debt-financed public expenditure as a stimulus to growth.

It was this feature of financial expansion and proliferation, and its role as an alternative to the increasingly restricted opportunities for productive investment in the stagflationary environment of the post-1960s, that defined the new system. In time, the much faster growth of finance weakened its link with the real economy. In the first instance the growth of finance was based on an expansion of the volume of credit assets created against real goods and assets, and on derivative financial assets aimed at reducing the risk associated with the holding of any given real asset. But soon the financial sector began to create multiple layers of derivative financial assets with their value having little to do with the real assets they were ostensibly related to, even if at some point far removed. It was this conversion of the financial sector into a factory producing financial products that allowed for the rapid rise in the ratios of financial assets to GDP, financial assets to real assets and financial profits to total profits. The rapid growth and proliferation of finance were facilitated by the fact that investments in financial assets were leveraged or financed with debt.

Associated with this expansion and diversification of financial activity were multiple sources through which financial players earned incomes. The most obvious was of course the many forms in which interest income was generated and transferred to those who held the right to those incomes. A second was the large fee and commission incomes earned by

financial players for facilitating transactions, designing contracts, manufacturing financial products, ensuring contract
adherence and arbitrating disputes. A third was the return
earned in the form of capital gains when financial asset prices
rose and these inflated values could be converted to near-
money in liquid markets, providing the purchasing power to
acquire goods, real assets and labour power. The size of these
returns could be large because the expansion of the financial sector was driven by leveraged investments financed with
borrowed capital that was many multiples of the own capital
of investors. Money capital serving as interest-bearing capital
was being allocated not only to finance productive investment
but to further financial investment, and that chain could be
extended so long as the activity of finance and the actions
of market-friendly central bankers ensured the availability of
substantial and cheap liquidity.

This form of restructuring has transformed capitalism
hugely, relative to the way it looked and functioned in Marx's
time. Marx's *Capital* was written in the Age of Industry.
Today, we live in the Age of Finance. As noted earlier, finance,
insurance and real estate account for high shares of total
value added in the United Kingdom (UK), United States of
America (USA) and Germany.[1] More significantly, financial
profits account for a rising share of total profits in the USA
and other developed economies. Meanwhile finance capital has spread globally, radiating from the financial centres
of metropolitan capitalism to the underdeveloped countries,

---

[1] Figures from *OECD Factbook: 2015–16*, available in OECD.
Stat at http://stats.oecd.org/. Value added in the Information and
Communication sector stood at 6 per cent in the UK and US, and 5
per cent in Germany.

and not just the so-called 'emerging markets'. No opportunity for financial profits is to be left unexploited.

Thus, finance today is very different from the times in which Marx wrote his seminal treatise, when credit assets were the main form of financial assets and banking the overwhelmingly dominant financial activity. In a supplementary note to *Capital*, Volume 3, Engels underlined the substantial expansion of stock exchange activity as compared to Marx's treatment of it.[2] A century later, when all regulations placed on finance during and after the Great Depression of the 1930s started to be lifted, there began a massive proliferation of financial activity that made the stock exchange itself only one minor location for non-banking financial activities undertaken by financial firms that were directly or indirectly engaged in a whole host of financial markets. So, while Marx looked at many features of the growth of money and finance in capitalism as it evolved till the last quarter of the nineteenth century, the face and shape of finance then were very different from what they are today.

The Profits of Finance

This does create a problem as to how we approach and apply Marx's understanding of the source of financial profit and the manner of its extraction. Marx was very clear that under capitalism surplus value was extracted through the productive consumption of labour power, in combination with whatever constant capital was required for the activity concerned. This was because the difference between the use value of labour

---

[2] Friedrich Engels, 'Supplement to *Capital, Volume Three*: The Stock Exchange' [1894], in Karl Marx, *Capital, Volume 3*, Moscow: Progress Publishers, 1967, pp. 908–10.

power to the capitalist (or its application for a full and elastic labour day) and the exchange value of that labour power (the wage) is the surplus that gets embodied in the commodity produced. Whatever role money capital and financial intermediaries had, the returns they received could only be a share of that surplus. Much of Marx's discussion was geared to examining the different roles money capital assumed and the ways in which it managed to extract a return from its activities. But in the course of that examination there developed various tensions in the analysis, in response to which Marx appears to have extended the frontiers of his understanding.

When elaborating his core arguments, Marx was at pains to show that money, exchange and circulation distract attention from the real source of surplus value. So, in the 'analysis of the primary form of capital, the form in which it determines the economic organization of modern society', he 'entirely left out of consideration' what he described as 'its well-known and so to speak antediluvian forms, merchant's capital and usurer's capital'.[3] That is, as discussed in my first lecture, besides locating their operations as subordinate functions in the realm of circulation where surplus value was only realized, he attempted to relegate them to the primitive phases of capitalism. But since merchants and moneylenders must, after all, profit to exist, and the money they withdraw as a result of their activity from the market must exceed that which was first advanced, the means to that profit needed to be identified. In Marx's view, the only way in which that profit can emerge is if they manage to extract a surplus from their transactions in the sphere of circulation. In the case of mer-

[3] Karl Marx, *Capital, Volume 2* (*Das Kapital* series, Book 2), Penguin Books, Kindle edition, 1978, pp. 265–66.

chant's capital, this occurs either because it offers a set of value services needed for the valorization of capital (such as storage and/or transportation) or because of the ability to ensure unequal exchange. Merchant's capital in its pure form, according to Marx, 'appears to be an impossibility, as long as equivalents are exchanged'. So the form M–C–M', buying in order to sell dearer, 'is at its purest in genuine merchant's capital'.[4]

Matters are even more deviant in the case of usurer's capital. In the case of merchant's capital,

> the money which is thrown upon the market and the augmented money which is withdrawn from the market, are at least mediated through a purchase and a sale, through the movement of circulation. In usurer's capital the form M–C–M' is reduced to the unmediated extremes M–M', money which is exchanged for more money, a form incompatible with the nature of money and therefore inexplicable from the standpoint of the exchange of commodities.[5]

Appropriating Profits from Outside of Production

Marx's understanding of usurer's capital was that it was a primitive form based essentially on the extraction of absolute surplus value. Thus, he argued:

> The distinctive character of the *formal* subsumption of labour under capital appears at its sharpest if we compare it to situations in which capital is to be found in certain specific, subordinate functions, but where it has not emerged as the direct purchaser of labour and as the immediate owner of the process

---

[4] Ibid.
[5] Ibid., p. 267.

of production, and where in consequence it has not yet succeeded in becoming the dominant force, capable of determining the form of society as a whole. In India, for example, the capital of the userer advances raw materials or tools or even both to the immediate producer in the form of money. The exorbitant interest which it attracts, the interest which, irrespective of its magnitude, it extorts from the primary producer, is just another name for surplus-value. It transforms its money into capital by extorting unpaid labour, surplus labour, from the immediate producer. But it does not intervene in the process of production itself, which proceeds in its traditional fashion, as it always had done.[6]

There are two aspects to this argument that need to be noted. The first is the recognition that money capital can manage to extract surplus value outside the sphere of production, and that this can be in the form of absolute surplus value when capital subordinates production as is and does not transform it. Second, the view that this happens only at the stage when capitalism is still emergent and has not seized the process of production. But when performing this parasitic role, it does pave the way for such seizure. This form of extraction of surplus value very often leads to the expropriation of peasants and petty producers, because they are forced to sell their meagre assets to the userer to service their debt, leaving the producer bereft of the means of production and with no commodity to sell other than his or her labour power. This too was, for Marx, a part of the process of 'primitive' accumulation.

As I have discussed earlier, when we go beyond the clas-

[6] Ibid., Appendix: 'Results of the Immediate Process of Production', pp. 1021–23.

sic ground of capitalism in England, the evidence suggests that these practices and tendencies continue to prevail in different forms through the history of world capitalism and even today. This implies that, when necessary and if possible, finance can extract its share of surplus by using means that do not require the mediation of production. The source of constantly enhanced value must be production, but the appropriation of that surplus could be both through production and outside it. This is all the more possible if profits accruing to money capital take the many forms I had referred to at the beginning of this lecture.

Finance and Speculation

Of course, Marx did not end his discussion of money and finance with this reference to the antediluvian forms of merchant's and userer's capital. Rather, that discussion features in Marx's analysis of capitalism at different levels. To start with, he recognized that with the development of circulation under capitalism, borrowing and lending, and debtors and creditors emerge, as money takes on the function of means of payment besides its functions as a measure of value and means of circulation. With credit being a widespread feature in the process of circulation, *settlements systems* emerge that cancel out implicitly reciprocal payments and require actual circulation of the means of payment only to balance the rest. The greater the concentration of amount of payments that can be settled in one place, the lower would be the amount of the means of payment in circulation.

The proliferation of debt paves the way for the emergence of credit money, since certificates of debt soon circulate by transferring the debts to others as a substitute for money.

Credit becomes tradeable. Besides facilitating transactions that are separated in time and space (such as the purchase of cotton for production of cloth, and the production and realization of the value of cloth through, say, the 'long' trade with India), this role for credit money soon results in a chain of debt. In Marx's words:

> By and large, money now functions only as means of payment, i.e. commodities are not sold for money, but for a written promise to pay at a certain date. For the sake of brevity, we can refer to all these promises to pay as bills of exchange. Until they expire and are due for payment, these bills themselves circulate as means of payment; and they form the actual commercial money. To the extent that they ultimately cancel each other out, by the balancing of debts and claims, they function absolutely as money, even though there is no final transformation into money proper.[7]

As these instruments proliferate, intermediaries in the form of banks, for example, take over the credit system, aggregating capital that allows for provision of cheaper credit on the larger scale demanded by a flourishing capitalist system and mediating the flow of credit money.

This build-up of finance is, in Marx's view, amplified by the fact that it is inevitably associated with speculation, which results in credit creation far in excess of that needed for facilitating circulation.

> It is the object of banking to give facilities to trade, and whatever gives facilities to trade gives facilities to speculation. Trade and

---

[7] Karl Marx, *Capital* (*Das Kapital* series, Book 3), Penguin Books, Kindle edition, 1981, pp. 524–25.

speculation are in some cases so nearly allied, that it is impossible to say at what precise point trade ends and speculation begins. . . . Wherever there are banks, capital is more readily obtained, and at a cheaper rate. The cheapness of capital gives facilities to speculation, just in the same way as the cheapness of beef and of beer gives facilities to gluttony and drunkenness.[8]

Fictitious Capital

Marx holds that money operating in this manner in the sphere of circulation gives rise to 'fictitious' capital because, in the words of one contemporary observer (Bosanquet):

> It is impossible to decide what part arises out of real bona fide transactions, such as actual bargain and sale, or what part is fictitious and mere accommodation paper, that is, where one bill of exchange is drawn to take up another running, in order to raise a fictitious capital, by creating so much currency.[9]

This capital is fictitious also because it confuses money and capital.

> The banker has grown so accustomed to figuring as distributor of the available social capital in the money form (distributing it in loans) that any function in which he hands out money appears to him as a loan. . . . If the bank grants the client a loan simply on his personal credit, without any security on his part, the matter is clear. He receives without condition an advance of a certain value in addition to the capital that he previously applied. He receives it in the money form; not just money, but money capital. But if the advance is made against securities,

---

[8] Ibid., pp. 525–32.
[9] Ibid., p. 526.

etc., which have to be deposited with the bank, it is an advance in the sense that money is paid to him under condition of its repayment, but it is not an advance of capital. For these securities also represent capital, and moreover a higher amount than the advance. The recipient thus receives less capital value than he deposits; and this is in no way an acquisition of extra capital for him. He does not undertake the transaction because he needs capital, but rather because he needs money.[10]

If money capital parading as capital but not supporting real transactions or providing additional capital for accumulation is fictitious, then much of modern-day finance will qualify as fictitious, especially capital invested in asset-backed securities and derivatives of other kinds. Modern economies seem to be flooded, even if not dominated, by assets that would qualify as fictitious capital in Marx's terms. The role of many new instruments is to facilitate the trading of risk, and not the debt from which the risk is detached. Whether this makes these assets all representative of fictitious capital is an issue I return to.

Meanwhile, in Marx, the sheer expansion of circulation leads to the separation of money (or finance) capital which facilitates monetary circulation from that used to gain command over commodities and hire labour power to generate surplus value. In its modern incarnation one independent role for finance appears as that of 'money-dealing capital', which acquires autonomy while performing specific operations involving movements outside the sphere of production. In that role it appears as a 'now independent part of the industrial capital in the course of its reproduction process'.[11]

---

[10] Friedrich Engels' editorial note in ibid., pp. 558–59.
[11] Marx, *Capital* (*Das Kapital* series, Book 3), p. 431.

Money-dealing in its pure form, payments and settlements, exchange business, etc., is separate from the credit system, and facilitates the monetary circulation needed for and associated with commodity circulation. This capital, therefore, represents 'on a diminished scale the additional capital which the merchants and industrial capitalists would otherwise have to advance for this purpose themselves'.[12] So, 'the mass of money capital which the money dealers operate with is the circulating money capital of the merchants and industrialists', and 'their profit is simply a deduction from surplus value, since they are dealing only with values already realized'.[13]

Interest-bearing Capital

However, Marx distinguishes between these 'money dealers' – or pure financial players of that time – and the payments made to them, and interest-bearing capital-lending to earn interest under capitalism. In the hands of the money capitalist, the money and means of payment is 'potential' capital, and in the hands of the capitalist engaged in production, it is 'functioning' capital. The former capital bears interest; the latter generates profit which is partly paid out to interest-bearing capital and the balance is retained as the profit of enterprise. The growing role for money capital as an independent form in the hands of independently functioning financial intermediaries soon affects the capital destined to finance production. The borrowing and lending of money become the special business of some money dealers. They appear as middlemen between the actual lenders of money capital and the borrowers. This

[12] Ibid., p. 438.
[13] Ibid.

concentrates loan capital in the hands of a few financial intermediaries, mainly banks, who are the ones to deal with the
borrowers.[14]

Overall,

> money – taken here as the independent expression of a sum
> of value, whether this actually exists in money or commodities
> – can be transformed into capital, and through the transforma-
> tion it is turned from a given, fixed value into a self-valorizing
> value capable of increasing itself. It produces profit, i.e it enables
> the capitalist to extract and appropriate for himself a certain
> quantity of unpaid labour, surplus product and surplus value.
> In this way the money receives, besides the use-value which it
> possesses as money, an additional use value, namely the ability
> to function as capital. *Its use-value here consists precisely in the
> profit it produces when transformed into capital.* In this capacity
> of potential capital, as means to the production of profit, it
> becomes a commodity, but a commodity of a special kind. Or
> what comes to the same thing, capital becomes a commodity.

So, if a proprietor pays a lender a portion of the profit thus
produced, what he pays for with this is 'the use-value of its
capital function'. The part of the profit paid in this way is
interest, 'which is nothing but a particular name, a special
title, for a part of the profit which the functioning capitalist
has to pay to the capital's proprietor, instead of pocketing it
himself'.[15]

Thus Marx's focus here sees the restoration of the link
between the independent money capitalist and production,
through the division of surplus into profit and interest. Yet

[14] Ibid., p. 528.
[15] Ibid., p. 460.

there is much that is being concealed. Profit of enterprise as a category appears as payment to the entrepreneur for the 'work done' as functioning capitalist, and interest earned as a property stemming from the ownership of capital. This separation of capital as property bearing interest, as against capital as function earning profits, results in profit of enterprise not standing as an antithesis to wages, or capital as function not being primarily seen as standing in opposition to and exploiting labour, but of profit forming an antithesis with interest.

This is an illusion. Marx is still clear that surplus value, whether it takes the form of profits of enterprise or interest, must be mediated by capitalist production:

> It is utter nonsense to suggest that all capital could be transformed into money capital without the presence of people to buy and valorize the means of production, i.e. the form in which the entire capital exists, apart from the *relatively small part existing in money*. Concealed in this idea, moreover, is the still greater nonsense that capital could yield interest on the basis of the capitalist mode of production without functioning as productive capital, i.e. without creating surplus value, of which interest is simply one part; that the capitalist mode of production could proceed on its course without capitalist production. If an inappropriately large number of capitalists sought to transform their capital into money capital, the result would be a tremendous devaluation of money capital and a tremendous fall in the rate of interest; many people would immediately find themselves in the position of being unable to live on their interest and thus compelled to turn themselves back into industrial capitalists.[16] (Emphasis added)

---

[16] Ibid., p. 501.

There are, however, two issues here that bear separation. One is the recognition that money capital assumes many autonomous forms, and finds ways of appropriating even if not generating surplus value while engaging in activities that involve no mediation of production. The second is the notion that the illusion, created by the expansion of finance, that money can beget money is merely a form of fetishism. In Volume 3 of *Capital* Marx notes:

> In the form of interest-bearing capital, capital appears immediately in this form, unmediated by the production and circulation processes. Capital appears as a mysterious and self-creating source of interest, of its own increase. The thing (money, commodity, value) is now already capital simply as a thing; the result of the overall reproduction process appears as a property devolving on a thing in itself; it is up to the possessor of money, i.e. of commodities in their ever-exchangeable form, whether he wants to spend this money as money or hire it out as capital. In interest-bearing capital, therefore, this automatic fetish is elaborated into its pure form, self-valorizing value, money breeding money, and in this form it no longer bears any marks of its origin. The social relation is consummated in the relationship of a thing, money, to itself.[17]

This, according to Marx, also creates the *illusion* that accumulation has no limits.

> The identity of surplus-value and surplus labour sets a qualitative limit to the accumulation of capital: the total working day, the present development of the productive forces and population, which limits the number of working days that can be

---

[17] Ibid., p. 516.

simultaneously exploited. But if surplus-value is conceived in the irrational form of interest, the limit is only quantitative, and beggars all fantasy.[18]

So, it is not just that surplus value is generated in production; it is also that the proliferation of credit money and other forms of speculative finance is in part fictitious and conceals the real antagonism inherent in capitalist production.

The focus on these extremely important features of money capital meant that Marx spent little time addressing the tension in *Capital* itself between the recognition of the rapid pace of expansion and proliferation of finance, and the notion that this is insubstantial, is not central to the generation of surplus value, and is in some senses an illusion and a form of fetishism. The tension in Marx's analysis is reflected in the fact that while he gave primacy to extraction of surplus value in production, he had to recognize the then just emerging complexities in the world of money and finance, which result in the appropriation of various functions in 'the circuit of industrial capital' by independent forms of money capital. This makes money capital crucial to the process of production and appropriation of surplus value, to the 'unity of production and circulation', and can vastly increase the share of aggregate profits accruing to money capital. The problem is that, as Marx himself saw it, as long as financial assets are liquid or can be sold in functioning markets for forms of immediate purchasing power, and the value of money is stable, they can be used to purchase commodities including labour power of an equivalent value. And those commodities can be put to use to generate surplus value. So their value is not all illusion.

[18] Ibid., p. 522.

To treat that capital as fictitious, then, is to ignore the role it can play in accumulation, if it chooses to.

The Age of Finance

These possibilities are amplified in the Age of Finance. If the development or evolution of capitalism involves handlers of money capital assuming multiple roles as money dealers, credit intermediaries, money capitalists and banks, more recent transitions that generate a whole world of financial dealers engaged in handling money capital invested in financial assets to exploit not just interest and fee income, but also capital gains, where investments appreciate and wealth begets more wealth without the intervention of commodities or circulation, can be seen as an intensification of that trend. However, instead of independent money capital retaining a link with production, it appears to feed on itself. The divergence between real and financial accumulation seems to widen.

One issue is whether the surpluses earned by finance capital are being generated in the financial sector rather than being appropriated through it. Given the understanding of the source of surplus value, it cannot be argued that this surplus originates in the financial sphere, or in circulation. But it is possible that the surplus is appropriated outside of and without the mediation of production, as was true of usurer's capital, and often in the form of absolute surplus value.

An extreme example of this is the present-day world of and fascination with 'inclusive finance'. It is in the nature of modern finance that it seeks to subordinate all realms of economic activity to it, so as to extract some surplus from them either as interest or in the form of foreclosed assets. So, private finance in a neoliberal world does not walk away from the bottom of the pyramid, even in rural areas, but finds new ways of subordinating its constituents. To 'reach' small enterprises, marginal farmers and poor borrowers, innovations of various kinds have been experimented with. Some are obvious, such as the use of business correspondents and banking facilitators as conduits for credit in locations where it does not make sense to establish brick-and-mortar banking facilities. Since they are local, these agents are better informed about their clients and more capable of gathering the information needed for viable lending. These agents deliver loans to the primary borrowers and are, in turn, supported with lines of credit from the banks, which reach credit to small borrowers in the process. Loans are not only for productive purposes but are used to finance some part of consumption expenditure or special needs such as emergency health expenditure. But the interest rates often compare with those charged by usurious moneylenders. What is extracted here is absolute surplus value by squeezing out a share of the meagre earnings of those who choose to smoothen their consumption using access to these financial services.

The other route to these borrowers is through the reliance on micro-finance companies. In the world of micro-finance, group-lending or the joint liability mechanism provides an implicit loan guarantee and promises high recovery. Having formed itself through self-selection, the group tends to be more capable (as a collective) of assessing the probability of default on borrowing by individual borrowers. In addition, peer pressure, driven by the fact that individual defaults affect the credibility of the group as a whole, ensures higher rates of recovery. Banks lend directly to these groups, or do so through the intermediation of a micro-finance institution (MFI).

These institutional innovations have been backed by

'pure' financial innovations such as securitization drawn from the world of 'macro finance'. This helps enlarge the volume of credit that can be profitably delivered to those who need to be financially included. The logic of this system is often hard to understand. Loans of this kind given to small and poor borrowers are more prone to default, given the economic condition of many micro-borrowers, as well as the evidence that borrowers take on loans from multiple MFIs and/or use loans from one to pay off dues to the other. The only way this trend can be explained is that lenders expect that there are assets available which can be seized in case of large-scale default – a form of primitive accumulation that transforms financial wealth into real wealth.

Financial Accumulation vs Real Accumulation

The much faster relative expansion of the 'size of finance' relative to real wealth in contemporary capitalism also gives the former far more autonomy than Marx envisaged. This makes it far more difficult to explain. Marx recognized that the expansion of interest-bearing capital results in a degree of independence for money capital. He saw that money capital gives command over labour, but did not extend this to a full analysis of the relation between financial and real accumulation. So long as the market for financial assets is liquid and the value of money is stable, illusory gains do give command over real assets.

In his time, Marx sought a resolution to the problem of the observed divergence between real and financial asset accumulation in the role he attributed to crises that are inevitable when this rise of finance reaches unsustainable levels. Crises result in an unwinding of unsustainable credit and a collapse in the value of financial assets. These crises of overproduction, while occurring because of the antagonistic nature of capitalist production, are partly a result of the growth of finance, of credit driving the system to its limits. This is because

> credit offers the individual capitalist, or the person who can pass as a capitalist, an absolute command over the capital and property of others, within certain limits, and, through this, command over other people's labour. It is disposal over social capital, rather than his own, that gives him command over social labour. The actual capital that someone possesses, or is taken to possess by public opinion, now becomes simply the basis for a superstructure of credit.[19]

The argument is that the credit system, by allowing those other than owners of capital control over 'social capital' in order to apply it to production and speculation, stretches the process of expanded reproduction to its limits. They are therefore willing to

> proceed quite unlike owners who, when they function themselves, anxiously weigh the limits of their private capital. This only goes to show how the valorization of capital founded on the antithetical character of capitalist production permits actual free development only up to a certain point, which is constantly broken through by the credit system.

But this also means that credit precipitates the violent crises implicit in this contradictory social formation.[20]

In contemporary capitalism, however, even if the accumulation of finance capital leads to a crisis, it does not neces-

[19] Ibid., p. 570.
[20] Ibid., p. 574.

sarily wipe out all past capital gains. One reason for this is that a financial crisis threatens to freeze the payments and settlements system and close the credit pipeline, both of which are crucial for the circuit of capital and the functioning of capitalism. The 'externalities' of a financial crisis are too significant for the state to ignore. In the event, in all major crises involving a crisis of the financial system, governments and central banks intervene to restore stability and profits in the financial system by injecting tax payers' money, or by socializing losses.

In fact, across crises, the rising floor – set to the value of wealth accumulated in the financial sector – raised the share of financial assets to real wealth substantially. Thus, financial speculation of this kind delivered substantial profits and constituted, therefore, another mode of capital accumulation for individual capitals. At least a part of this wealth was paper wealth and illusionary. When the bubble burst, much of this 'capital' vanished. But that value was quickly rebuilt with the aid of the state. And the resulting financial overhang appropriated and redistributed in favour of finance capital, through multiple means, a range of surpluses generated elsewhere in the economy.

But this divergence between real wealth which can be 'commanded' by finance, and financial wealth generated through multiple means, cannot remain unbridged, for in order that finance can command real wealth, such wealth of equivalent value must exist. If the 'production' of financial wealth occurs faster than that of real wealth available to be traded in the market, then new sources of real wealth must be found. One source is of course through privatization of public sector assets, which makes available wealth accumulated through the investment of social surplus to private capital. Another is through privatization of common property resources and by making them means for the self-expansion of value: land, water, forests, spectrum, and perhaps the ocean, hitherto treated as outside the domain of private ownership, are converted into assets that can be privately owned and traded, enhancing the quantum of real wealth that can be commanded. Finally, the operations of finance can be used as a means to expropriate assets that can then be commanded by financial capital, as happens with the so-called 'inclusive finance' of today.

What this suggests is that the divergence in the rates of growth of financial and real assets can remain large, and even continue rising, so long as the state presents itself as a site for primitive accumulation, means of surplus appropriation in the form of absolute surplus value can be found by capital standing outside production, and real assets are continuously appropriated and released to back the financial wealth which is only partly eroded in the course of capitalism's periodic crises. In this sense, not all of capital is fictitious so long as this process can continue. It is only a claim on real wealth that must be unearthed or expropriated. The process will continue so long as finance capitalism dominates. Since capitalism does not collapse, the process can continue till either another crisis restructures capitalism in ways that undermine finance, like the New Deal did, or political developments lead to the transcendence of capitalism.

4

Marx's *Capital* and the
Current Crisis of Capitalism

Over the last three lectures I have, when returning to *Capital* after 150 years of the publication of Volume I, sought in its method and substance formulations and insights relevant to an understanding of contemporary capitalism. From the vantage point of 2017, a feature of capitalism that is a focus of attention is the specific form of the intense and prolonged crisis that hit capitalism at its core in 2007, and plagues it globally even to this day. This was and is in all senses a 'general crisis', affecting all sectors and, viewing capitalism as a world system, all areas.

But it would be wrong to see this crisis in isolation. The transformation of capitalism in the years after the end of the Golden Age has increased the fragility of the system considerably. If we consider the US economy, for example, before being mired in the current crisis it had not just been subject to periodic cycles of crisis, but had experienced the savings and loans crisis of the late 1980s and early 1990s, and the dot-com bust of the early 2000s. So, the 2007–08 crisis and the recession that followed must be seen as a culmination of tendencies that had made the system more prone to violent disruptions. What we need to fathom are the factors that gave rise to this fragility which culminated in an intense crisis in 2007–08.

As I had noted in the second lecture on order and anarchy under capitalism, Marx had no single, overarching theory of crisis. He points instead to a number of tendencies that, given the antagonistic and anarchic nature of capitalism, lead to crises of overproduction or, at the other pole, underconsumption. There are, however, counteracting tendencies operative at all times, and the strength of these tendencies determines whether a crisis actually occurs and its intensity. Besides, when crises occur, and especially when they are intense, capital modifies its environment and restructures its operations, weakening the impact of certain causative factors till such time as these modifications are effective. These offsetting tendencies operate even in Marx's conceptual context of a closed and fully capitalist economy. When the system is opened and allowed to interact with pre-capitalist formations within and outside national boundaries, the means to postpone or resolve crises are substantially more, as markets, sources of raw materials and surpluses extracted in various forms help mitigate the effects and consequences of antagonism and anarchy.

Understanding an actual crisis, therefore, requires applying the apparatus Marx has given us, to identify the factors that create the conditions for such a crisis – factors that are shaped during periods of normalcy or even prosperity. A fundamental problem in capitalism is that, since it is a system locked into the logic of the self-expansion of value by extracting surplus value and directing it to expanded reproduction, the process of accumulation is self-propelled. At the same time, competition between capitals, and the need to prevent wages from rising at the expense of profit, drive investments in improved means of production that raise productivity and help to constantly replenish the reserve army of unemployed labour. Accumulation proceeds, but wages and employment do not keep pace. As a result, overproduction (relative to demand) prevents surplus from being realized as profits, which in turn leads to a disruption of the process of expanded reproduction. In parallel, the anarchic nature of capitalism, involving uncoordinated investment decision-making, ensures that inter-sectoral balance conditions required for expanded reproduction are periodically violated, resulting in disruption of production.

The Role of the Periphery

These tendencies towards crises were, since the inception of capitalism and the rise of late nineteenth-century imperialism, counteracted by capitalism's subordination and exploitation of the underdeveloped and less developed regions of the world. As has been underlined, Marx did recognize and discuss this elsewhere, but paid less attention to it in *Capital* because of his focus on capitalism as a closed system. In the period since the Second World War, despite decolonization, neo-colonial relationships ensured that this relationship of subordination of the periphery continued, explaining to a substantial extent the resilience of the capitalist mode. Not surprisingly, increased economic integration of far-flung regions of global capitalism was a part of the restructuring that followed the crisis of the 1960s.

The domination and subordination implicit in this relationship are starkly illustrated by the fact that major developments that seemed to redress the unequal international balance of economic power soon lost their significance. Both the oil shocks of the 1970s, following the nationalization of oil resources and the formation of OPEC (Organization of Petroleum Exporting Countries), and the shift of global manufacturing production to a few developing countries that turned successful exporters, which reshaped the international division of labour, seemed to give the less developed countries a larger share of the world's surpluses. But in time these advantages were either dissipated, or, given the overall deflation in the world economy, the surpluses earned by the developing countries through these developments were diverted from productive accumulation to the global financial system controlled in the metropolitan countries.

Further, in another illustration of the contradictory character of the capitalist system, the process of integration has also increased the instability of capitalism. The international expansion triggered by the process of resolution of the 1960s' crisis saw increased sourcing of goods and services from and relocation of production to less developed countries with a large and cheap reserve army of unemployed labour. Metropolitan capital has been increasingly globalized as policies that prise open the markets for goods, services, labour and finance were promoted across the world in the name of liberalization and economic 'reform'. One consequence of the reordering of global production that resulted was an increase in global trade imbalances. With some countries turning out to be the dominant producers and exporters of manufactured goods and primary commodities, and others their consumers and importers, the global trade balance reflected differential levels of surpluses and deficits. Cross-border flows of finance helped to restore balance, but flows may not match requirements in all periods, resulting in more frequent disruptions of the system of reproduction in individual countries because of balance of payments problems.

On the other hand, global sourcing through purchase and production, by expanding the reserve army of labour available to the now globalized metropolitan capital, directly addressed the issue of any squeeze of profits as a result of wage increases. It also indirectly served the objective of maximizing surplus extraction by keeping wages in the metropolitan countries low, because of competition from labour abroad and the fragmentation of labour markets with precarious employment conditions at home. In addition, since it was the more labour-intensive segments of manufacturing that were relocated abroad, employment growth was limited and unemployment high. Finally, policy measures aimed at rendering labour markets 'flexible' were used to prevent pre-existing structures from being obstacles to their transformation. A consequence of these trends was that they rendered technological change and innovation in the metropolitan core less significant from the point of view of preventing a decline in the rate of profit. The relevant reserve army of labour was enlarged and replenished even without labour-displacing technical change.

The Influence of Finance

This proved useful because the other component of capitalist restructuring in the years after the late 1960s was, as discussed in the last lecture, the growing importance of finance. This does not suppress the appetite for accumulation inherent in capitalism, but shifts the focus of such accumulation to the financial sector and to financial wealth, as a means to unearthing and acquiring real wealth. This changes the nature and pace of development of the productive forces. Assessed in the light of Marx's discussion in *Capital*, the rise of finance has eroded the dynamism of capitalism by reshaping the role of productive forces and stunting technological change in the system. It also erodes the ability of collective labour to galvanize the productive forces through articulation of the antagonism between labour and capital.

This is partly because under contemporary capitalism, in the search for profit from capital gains, especially the appreciation of the value of financial assets, economic activity outside the financial sector tends to be shaped by finance. Which sectors turn out to be the sunrise sectors in the economy; which firms flourish, and which survive and grow; which firms shut down, or are merged or amalgamated with others; and which 'technologies' tend to get showcased – all of these are shaped, often unbeknownst to us, by finance. One illustration of this is the growing importance of 'start-ups' in the 'new' capitalism. Certain firms experimenting with certain technologies are chosen as the target for financial bets. Few of these survive, even if they are extremely well funded with money capital (suitably named 'venture' capital) in their early years. International experience shows that most of them die early; some survive briefly and then fade away, like Netscape, AOL and Yahoo, but do deliver significant money gains to shareholders and generate fortunes for their promoters; and a very small number, like Google and Apple, go on to become leading firms, the promoters of which join the world's ever-richer richest. Yet, for the money (venture) capitalists, the gains made from the few successes are more than enough to wipe out the losses associated with the many failures and make them billionaires. Serving as mere interest-bearing capital loaned to functioning capital seems to generate a mere pittance. Being the equivalent of what Marx termed fictitious capital is a better bet.

Recognizable in this new regime of accumulation is a change in how technology is perceived. Technology in the era prior to the Age of Finance was largely a combination of 'hardware' and 'software' that used a certain set of specified capital goods, intermediates and components to undertake a planned production routine, to yield a product with a specific design, technical characteristics and use value within a defined organizational framework, like the factory. This allowed us to break down technology into segments such as materials technology, manufacturing technology, design technology and managerial technology. The last was clearly far less of a technology than the others. But technological change could involve improvements in any of these segments. A feature of technology in recent years is the growing importance of 'software' elements and managerial technology in the spectrum. Today's so-called 'technology majors' include the likes of Google (a search engine), Facebook (a social media platform), Amazon (an e-commerce firm) and Uber (an aggregator). This allows for both widening of the scope of innovation and an increase in the pace of obsolescence of technologies, providing a constant source of 'new, new things' on which finance can place its bets.

With wealth on the rise and manufacturing in decline in the leading metropolitan countries, the period of the rise of finance is also characterized by rapid expansion of the services economy and an increase in the gross domestic 'product' (GDP) generated from services. This is because of the specific way in which finance has moulded the use of information technology, allowing it to transform the organization of industries delivering products and those offering services, like commercial taxi services. These are innovative routes to profit but are by no means evidence of technological dynamism. In fact, the erosion of technological dynamism implicit in these tendencies points to a larger crisis due to which the progressive character of capitalism in its early stages is in decline. The relations that define the nature of surplus value extraction and the regime of accumulation under the capitalist mode in its contemporary form are proving to be major fetters on the productive forces.

This brings to the fore and intensifies other antagonisms characteristic of capitalism. As I have argued, the immanent logic of finance capital is that it seeks to beget more money from money, through multiple means of extracting absolute and relative surplus value. Some of these means involve the mediation of production but many do not. The result is a huge accumulation of financial wealth, waiting to be transformed into real wealth. In the process, however, the antagonism inherent is capitalism intensifies. Increases in income and wealth accrue largely to a few, resulting in huge increases in inequality. Inevitable in such a regime of accumulation, now reproduced on a global scale, is a tendency to overproduction and underconsumption. That antagonism asserts itself not just in periodic violent eruptions, but in a persisting environment of slow growth and deflation.

Finance and Crises under Capitalism

With the 2007–08 crisis occurring in what is here identified as the Age of Finance, the principal characteristics of which I have discussed in the previous lecture, it is to be expected that financial accumulation and its relationship with real accumulation will influence the features of the crisis and its causes. In fact, the narrative around the crisis that broke in 2007 was that it was initially a financial crisis which threatened the solvency of banks and financial firms, and eroded the value of financial assets. The 'externalities' or external effects of this on the real economy were seen as having precipitated the real economy crisis. But, while giving primacy to finance in driving real economy growth, this leaves unanswered the question of why, well after the crisis in the financial sector *per se* was resolved, the real economy crisis persists.

Of course, in Marx's time, the size and structure of the financial sector were such that while it mediated the various roles of money, it could not be seen as an important driver of crises of accumulation. Marx, who did see a connection between the cyclical movement of investment and production, and credit cycles, was not comfortable with arguments that traced the source of a crisis to finance, or, in his case, the credit superstructure. In a strong declaration of this position, he stated: 'The superficiality of political economy shows itself in the fact that it views the expansion and contraction of credit as the cause of the periodic alternations in the industrial cycle, whereas it is a mere symptom of them.'[1] To him cycles were an inherent characteristic of expanded reproduction under capitalism, with the process being disrupted when the factors driving accumulation could not be sustained.

It is, however, possible that in the course of the boom, the access to money capital is used to fuel the speculation that prosperity makes possible. Hence, when the boom ends, for reasons outside of the sphere of finance, those burdened with debt are doubly hurt. But the reasons why the boom ends lie elsewhere. Thus, discussing the 1847–48 crisis, Marx argued:

There was a dearth of money capital brought about by the

---

[1] Karl Marx, *Capital: A Critique of Political Economy* (*Das Kapital* series, Book 1), Penguin Books, Kindle edition, 1976, p. 786.

excessive size of operations, in comparison with the means available, and brought to a head by a disturbance in the reproduction process that resulted from the harvest failure, the over-investment in railways, overproduction particularly in cotton goods, swindling in the Indian and Chinese trade, speculation, excessive imports of sugar, and so on. What people who had bought corn at 120 shillings per quarter lacked, when the price fell to 60 shillings, was the 60 shillings too much which they had paid, and the corresponding credit for this in loans with the corn as security. It was in no way a lack of banknotes that prevented them from converting their corn into money at the former price of 120 shillings. The same with those who had imported too much sugar, which became unsaleable. The same with the gentlemen who had tied up their floating capital in railways and had found a replacement by conducting their 'legitimate' business on credit.[2]

A 'realization' problem caused the crisis, but when it occurred, those who had exploited the credit system for justifiable or speculative reasons found themselves trapped in a financial or debt crisis. A credit cycle accompanied the real cycle and intensified its effects, but it did not determine the actual economic cycle.

This role of money capital and its relationship with crises needs some modification, however, when we examine the role that finance capital came to play in the years after the end of the post-war Golden Age. As discussed, the crisis in the late 1960s and 1970s necessitated a restructuring of capitalism, and besides the forms it took as discussed above, it included

---

[2] Karl Marx, *Capital* (*Das Kapital* series, Book 3), Penguin Books, Kindle edition, 1981, pp. 550–51.

elements to address inflation, the banking crisis it gave rise to, and the deceleration in real economy growth which followed the contractionary response to inflation in the form of expenditure cuts and stringent monetary policy.

To start with, two kinds of tendencies developed to rein in inflation in the developed capitalist countries. One was a radical shift in favour of restricted public expenditure or contractionary fiscal policies in the metropolitan core and the peripheral underdeveloped countries, which depressed demand and held down the prices of primary commodities (including energy) and kept real wages stagnant. The other was the sourcing from or relocation to low-wage locations of manufacturing production that helped keep price increases low in metropolitan markets.

Secondly, the crisis in banking was sought to be resolved by permitting financial firms much greater flexibility in terms of operation, sourcing of capital and permitted investments. To that end, measures adopted since the 1930s to regulate financial markets in the Anglo-Saxon world were dismantled, allowing for an unbridled expansion of finance. The consequence was a huge expansion of financial assets with the nature and relative roles of pre-existing markets, institutions and instruments changing, and new institutions and instruments emerging. But underlying all this was a set of credit assets that were created in depository institutions, especially banks, and securities issued in equity and bond markets. These credit assets and primary securities were bundled into derivative assets. The derived securities were then packed, sliced and distributed further. And the possibility of loss from holding those securities was insured for a price varying with contractual terms. This was the edifice based on which massive financial profits were made.

Riding on a Credit Bubble

But if the edifice was built on credit assets and primary securities, increasing the volume of financial assets required increasing the volume and value of these primary assets. If we take credit assets, for example, the volume of debt created by the banking system must increase substantially to sustain the process of so-called 'financialization'. This debt was provided to finance corporate investments, housing investments of households, and a range of household expenditures varying from spending on purchase of automobiles and consumer durables to expenditure on education and other services. This generated demand more than made up for the fiscal conservatism and public expenditure cuts characteristic of the Age of Finance, and kept growth going. By replacing debt-financed public expenditure with debt-financed private expenditure, the 'community of finance' found a way to restore a modicum of growth even when mass incomes were frozen in the interest of enhancing profits. Growth was being driven by generating a private sector credit bubble.

To keep this process going, of growth riding on a credit bubble, the access to liquidity of the banking system needs to be substantial, and the interest rates at which they lend low enough to find and attract large numbers of borrowers. Both were ensured by the role given to monetary policy, now privileged over fiscal policy as the principal macroeconomic instrument. If inflation ruled high, the typical neo-liberal response – code-named 'inflation targeting' – was a tight money policy, with stringent controls on money supply and high interest rates. But in the deflationary environment that the new regime of accumulation put in place, inflation was low, so monetary policy could be loose and interest rates low.

The resulting infusion of liquidity into the system, and the speculation and carry trade that followed, resulted in asset price inflation. In the Age of Finance, when capital gains rather than profit, interest and rent are the main form of return for owners of assets, inflation in commodity prices is anathema, but asset price appreciation is a virtue. In the event, speculation thrived in assets markets, fuelled by easily available cheap credit, which generated a bubble of another sort. This too helped stimulate demand through the 'wealth effect', where capital appreciation, by making households feel richer, encourages debt-financed spending in the short run. Capitalism in the Age of Finance is moribund in a double sense: it places significant fetters on the advance of the productive forces, and it relies on speculative bubbles in credit and other financial markets as a means to growth.

However, even this moribund form of capitalism contained several contradictions that affected this strategy. One was the heightened probability of default. Since this process of growth driven by debt and speculation was based on giving credit to those whose incomes could not finance the expenditures they undertook, it increased the indebtedness of those who did not necessarily have the means to deliver the payments due on their debt. Even in the case of many who had current incomes to meet debt service commitments, there was no certainty that those incomes would be available through the entire term when payments fell due. A rising rate of default was inevitable. When the ratio of defaults to advances crosses a certain threshold, banks would hold back on providing further debt, undermining the principal driver of growth.

The second contradiction was that the demand generated by debt-financed spending was crucial to the employment and incomes of many borrowers. That set up a vicious feedback loop wherein, if default resulted in a credit squeeze, the number of defaulters could increase further and rapidly, since the credit needed to keep growth going and deliver incomes to cover debt service commitments would be lacking. The process of accumulation rides on a knife-edge.

Finally, as emphasized earlier, the whole regime of accumulation rests on a strategy of depressing the wages and incomes of petty and primary commodity producers to contain inflation, whereas owners of assets, especially financial assets, benefit from capital appreciation. The resulting inequality, by capping demand from a large section of the population, provides grounds for overproduction and underconsumption. When the debt bubble can no longer be sustained, the real investments triggered by this strategy could run ahead of demand, as it did.

The Role of the State

These features of the most recent crisis that has afflicted global capitalism indicate that the manner in which finance and the real economy are intertwined in the Age of Finance influences the regime of accumulation, the tendencies leading to crises and the factors that precipitate the crisis. This substantially enhanced role for finance, when compared with the capitalism that was the object of Marx's analysis in *Capital*, influences the response of the state to crises when they occur.

To start with, since finance presents itself as an engine of growth, the argument gains ground that 'saving finance' or 'saving the banks' must be a leading ingredient in any attempt at engineering a recovery. The difficulty, however, is that this alone is not enough. Even if insolvent or near-insolvent banks are returned to solvency by injection of capital by the state and infusion of liquidity by the central bank, they can return to profit only if business resumes. That is, they must find creditworthy borrowers with creditworthy projects that they can finance. This requires restoring the real economy to health as well, so as to spur demand and induce investment.

As discussed, an obvious instrument for this purpose, used with effect in the aftermath of the Great Depression, is substantially enhanced public expenditure. In the immediate period following the onset of the 2007 global financial crisis as well, public expenditure was significantly enhanced by governments across the globe. But soon a controversy arose over the mode of financing of this expenditure. Clearly, in the midst of a crisis, when demand is depressed, profits are eroded and asset prices are falling, taxation to finance enhanced state expenditure would be difficult to justify. So, in the short run, state expenditure has to be financed with borrowing. From the point of view of finance, the danger associated with debt-financed, autonomous public spending is that, if chosen as a soft option by governments, it could trigger inflation – as it did in the late 1960s. This danger is even greater if governments decide to finance expenditures aimed at providing basic social services and a modicum of social security to those who gain little from growth in the Age of Finance. Inflation is anathema to finance because it erodes the real value of financial assets and the real interest income they earn. So, debt-financed expenditures that (in its view) can trigger inflation are opposed by it.

But this should not constrain resort to such expenditure in the current environment, since most economies are experiencing low inflation or deflation. Yet, even relatively small increases in government deficits and public borrowing soon run up against strong criticism and opposition from representatives or spokespersons of finance capital. Besides the opposition to state spending because it legitimizes state action in a private enterprise world, there are other possible reasons underlying this criticism. One is that the preferred mode of financing government spending from the perspective of finance capital is the privatization of public assets. As I have argued in the previous lecture, as the value of financial wealth races ahead of real wealth in the system, new avenues for converting financial into real wealth must be found to validate the former and rid it of the stigma of being mere fictitious capital. If governments choose to hold on to existing real wealth owned by them and to finance new public wealth creation with debt, the access of the private sector to past and future real wealth is limited. The aim of private finance, therefore, would be to shrink public wealth, leading to opposition towards debt-financed public expenditure.

A similar limitation could arise within the realm of finance as well, because of the role of government securities as a near-zero-risk hedging option. Government securities issued to mobilize public debt are considered risk-free and highly liquid. But if governments flood the market with such securities a risk of default on the debts of at least some governments could arise, and trading in government securities may be less easy than otherwise. For these (and other) reasons, debt-financed public spending very often shrinks rather than expands during crises in the Age of Finance.

This is what happened two to three years after 2008. So long as debt was being incurred by governments largely to save financial firms, all objections to excessive public borrowing were buried. Problems arose when, having saved the banks and financial firms, governments turned their attention to restoring growth and strengthening safety nets for those who had been rendered unemployed and/or were hit badly by the crisis. At this point the traditional hostility of finance against government deficits and public debt came to the fore. In the event, governments were forced to drop their reliance on deficit spending. Since in the initial phases a large part of the deficit went to recapitalize the banks, the actual fiscal stimulus even during the short period it lasted was small. The system soon lost steam and sank back into recession.

Relying on the Monetary Lever

It is true that despite globalization, the world is still one populated with nation-states. The governments in all of them need not, it could be argued, follow the same strategy. But, as had become clear in the 1980s, if any single government resorts to a proactive fiscal policy while keeping its markets open to finance, the disapproval of finance can take the form of a disruptive flight of capital that precipitates a balance of payments and/or currency crisis. Hence, governments choose to abjure resort to fiscal stimuli. The fact that governments succumbed to the pressure not to use debt-financed fiscal spending as a means of stimulating a recovery made monetary policy measures such as liquidity infusion and interest rate reduction the principal instruments to combat recession and spur recovery. One important means to liquidity infusion was bond purchases by the central bank at relatively high prices. According to the *Financial Times* (16 August 2017), the six central banks that adopted policies of 'quantitative easing' – the US Federal Reserve, the European Central Bank, the Bank of Japan, the Bank of England, and the Swiss and Swedish central banks – now hold more than $15 trillion of assets, or more than four times the pre-crisis level. Of this, more than $9 trillion is in government bonds, amounting to one-fifth of the $46 trillion total outstanding debt owed by their governments. The rest consists of other bonds and securities. Overall, the US Federal Reserve's balance sheet rose from a little less than $1 trillion before the crisis to $4.5 trillion currently. Capital was made available at extremely low, near-zero interest rates. Once the crisis spread to Europe, this policy was adopted there as well.

Implicit in this dependence on monetary policy is the idea that private debt at low interest rates would substitute for public debt to revive demand and growth. That is, the idea is to use central bank action to revive the credit bubble that had gone bust. The problem is that this expected outcome is not being realized, partly because firms and households already overburdened with debt are not confident of raising earnings to levels needed to service additional debt. That is, neither does mere infusion of liquidity resolve the problem of default, foreclosure and bankruptcy, nor does monetary policy deliver the incomes needed to return indebted households and firms to a condition where they can meet their debt service commitments and begin borrowing again. The flip-side of this is that banks and other financial institutions are less willing to lend because of fear of default. Since monetary policy is directed at these institutions in the first instance, reliance on such policies does not deliver a recovery.

On the other hand, over-reliance on the monetary lever has had some bizarre effects. One is the movement of interest rates to negative territory, which reflects the desperation that has overcome governments which find that deep rate cuts have not had the desired effects of stalling the downturn and ensuring recovery. One form the tendency takes is for central banks to set their policy rates, which signal their monetary stance, below zero. If banks maintain deposits with the central banks, they are penalized by expropriating a part of that deposit rather than paying them interest. If banks borrow from the central banks, they are often rewarded with a subsidy. Thus, negative rates are the consequence of policy-makers betting on interest rate cuts to drive growth through multiple channels. To start with, they expect bank lending rates to come down and encourage households and firms to spend and/or invest more, raising demand. Second, investors not wanting to pay governments for holding their money are expected to turn to asset markets like the stock market. That would raise financial asset prices and trigger the oft-cited 'wealth effect'. With the value of paper or real assets rising, holders of those assets would be encouraged to spend more today rather than add further to accumulated wealth, spurring demand. Finally, since low and negative interest rates in a country would discourage foreign investors from investing in bonds and financial assets in the country concerned, the currency can depreciate, improving the competitiveness of exports.

The difficulty is that these expectations are not being realized. Households and firms that are still burdened with debt are wary about borrowing more, and banks are cautious of increasing their exposure to them even if pushed by the central bank. This could partly explain the thirst for government bonds that have driven their yields to turn negative as well. On the other hand, with all countries relying on interest rate cuts, the effective depreciation of currencies, while significant vis-à-vis the dollar, is only marginal vis-à-vis each other. That neutralizes the benefits of competitiveness from depreciation relative to the dollar, with little chance of an export boom.

Parallel to these developments is concern about the effect that negative rates can have on financial markets. They could trigger a shift to stocks away from bonds and set off a speculative spiral in stock markets. Negative rates are likely to adversely affect bank profits as well. While banks need to pay depositors a reasonable rate to attract their savings into deposits, the low interest environment and pressure to lend require them to cut the rates they charge their borrowers. The result is a squeeze on margins. The effect this could have on financial markets is still uncertain. In short, there are grounds to believe that while negative rates are the result of the ineffectiveness of interest rate reduction as a means to spur recovery, they can lead to financial instability.

Why, then, are central banks and governments opting for this unusual stance? In a famous 1943 essay on the 'Political Aspects of Full Employment',[3] the Polish economist Michal Kalecki had argued that if the rate of interest or income tax is reduced in a slump (to counter it) but not increased in the subsequent boom,

> the boom will last longer, but it must end in a new slump: one reduction in the rate of interest or income tax does not . . . eliminate the forces which cause cyclical fluctuations in a capitalist economy. In the new slump it will be necessary to reduce the rate of interest or income tax again and so on. Thus in the not too remote future, the rate of interest would have to be negative and income tax would have to be replaced by an income subsidy.

In the current context, the problem is not that a reduction of the interest rate during the slump, while triggering and elongating a boom, does not prevent the next slump from

[3] Michal Kalecki, 'Political Aspects of Full Employment' [1943], in *Selected Essays on the Dynamics of a Capitalist Economy*, Cambridge: Cambridge University Press, 1971, pp. 138–45.

occurring. The problem is that large reductions in policy interest rates when they were in positive territory did not counter
the slump. But since governments have forsaken completely
the option of relying on the fiscal lever to manoeuvre a recovery, they have no choice but to continue reducing interest
rates, which have finally entered negative territory. But that
too seems unlikely to trigger growth in the foreseeable future.
It is only increasing the prospects of another financial bust.

Implications

In sum, the rise to dominance of finance capital has under-
mined the ability of the state to return to the instruments
it used to sustain the recovery from the Great Depression
made possible by the Second World War, and turn it into
high growth. That instrument had been blunted by inflation
in the late 1960s and after. But now, the power and hostility
of finance limit the degree to which governments can resort
to it. As the presence and power of finance increase, therefore,
fiscal conservatism becomes the norm and austerity a recur-
rent policy recommendation. The result is persistence of the
crisis despite the huge effort in terms of liquidity infusion
resorted to by governments in the developed and underdeveloped countries.

Meanwhile, in the less developed countries, the invasion
by global finance facilitated by the surfeit of cheap liquidity increases instability massively. The destabilizing nature
of financial flows became clear with the debt crisis in Latin
America in the 1980s, and was driven home by the Southeast
Asian financial crisis in 1997. Over that period and since,
almost no less developed country has escaped being a victim of
an external crisis precipitated by footloose finance in search of

profit. In the case of Southeast Asia, even countries performing strongly, including so-called 'miracle' growth countries like South Korea, experienced major disruptions of economic activity, the effects of which are still visible. Recovery from the crisis did not mean a return to 'miracle' status. Instead, it was accompanied by significant acquisition, at deflated prices, of productive assets in these economies by foreign firms. It involved a substantial restructuring of the financial sector. It altered the nature of engagement with the world system of these economies, and their subordination by imperialism and global finance shows through in multiple ways. With the system being flooded with cheap liquidity, instability and subordination are only aggravated.

I had started this series of lectures saying that when we return to *Capital* 150 years after its first edition was published, an issue we must address is its resilience, belying the expectation of Marx (and Engels) at that time. I am ending this series by arguing that despite the hype that surrounds the activities of global finance, capitalism today is more moribund than ever, afflicted by a persisting low-intensity crisis and subject to violent disruptions of increasing periodicity. If yet capitalism survives, it is because economic factors alone do not ensure the transcendence of an exploitative system. Capitalism will not collapse under the weight of its own anarchy. It must be transcended through the action of social forces angered at the inhumanity of capitalism, and the unemployment and waste it perpetrates in order to enrich a miniscule minority. It is indeed true that the transformation of capitalism has shrunk and weakened the organized working class, the force that Marx and Engels expected will lead the movement for a new order. But that may be only telling us that the transition will not occur because of a gradual build-up of an opposition that would win when crises reveal that the system is rotten at the core. It will possibly be precipitated by events that are as unexpected and disruptive as crises themselves tend to be. But, however the movement to transcend capitalism is galvanized, it must be armed with its own critique of capitalism and driven by a vision of a new society. The method and substance of *Capital*, and the large body of other work that Marx, Engels and their successors have left us, definitely provide a basis for that critique and that vision.